Grade 5

Carson-Dellosa Publishing LLC
Greensboro, North Carolina

Credits
Content Editor: Kristina Biddle, M. Ed, NBCT
Copy Editor: Elise Craver

Visit *carsondellosa.com* for correlations to Common Core, state, national, and Canadian provincial standards.

Carson-Dellosa Publishing LLC
PO Box 35665
Greensboro, NC 27425 USA
carsondellosa.com

ISBN 978-1-4838-4170-0
02-281181151

Table of Contents

Introduction

Language Arts 4 Today: Daily Skill Practice is a comprehensive yet quick and easy-to-use supplement to any classroom language arts curriculum. This series will strengthen students' reading skills as they review comprehension, fluency, vocabulary, and decoding skills. Students' writing skills will improve as they practice parts of speech, grammar, and spelling.

This book covers 40 weeks of daily practice. Essential language arts skills are reviewed each day during a four-day period with an assessment of the skills practiced on the fifth day. Each week includes a fluency practice section, intended to be a quick one-minute activity that encourages fluency in reading and recognition of sight words. For more detailed fluency tips, see pages 5 and 6. The week concludes with a writing journal prompt.

Various skills and concepts are reinforced throughout the book through activities that align to the state standards. To view these standards, see the Standards Alignment Chart on page 7.

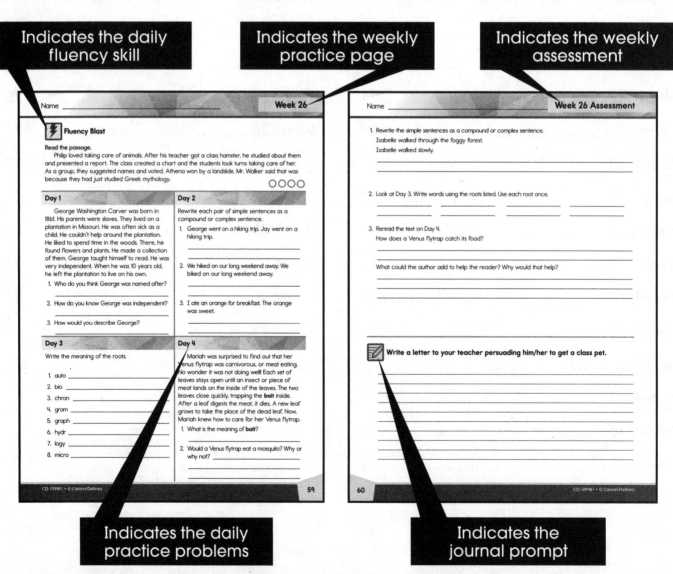

Indicates the daily fluency skill

Indicates the weekly practice page

Indicates the weekly assessment

Indicates the daily practice problems

Indicates the journal prompt

CD-104981 • © Carson-Dellosa

Developing Fluency

Fluency is the ability to read accurately, effortlessly, and with proper expression while comprehending the text. A growing number of studies have identified reading fluency as an important factor in student reading success.

The Four Components of Fluency

- *Accuracy* involves reading words correctly. Accuracy matters the most when the reader's mistakes change the meaning of the text.
- *Rate* is the ability to move through the text at the proper pace. Moving too fast or too slow through the text should not interfere with the reader's expression, voice, or comprehension.
- *Expression* is a reader's voice expression. Expression can indicate comprehension as the reader adjusts his voice to show the tone or mood of the text.
- *Phrasing* indicates the reader can move smoothly through the text in meaningful phrases with careful regard to punctuation.

Using the Fluency Blast

Students should read the weekly fluency blast passage (or sight words) for the week every day (excluding assessment day). They will then color one bubble for each reading. Use one or a combination of the following ways to read the passages (or sight words):

- Set a timer for one minute (or 30 seconds for faster readers). Have students read the passage and mark the last word read. Students should try to improve on the number of words read per minute each day.
- Allow students to read at their own pace each day.
- Students can read the passage while focusing on a particular word work skill such as marking the prefixes or suffixes in the passage.
- Have students read the passage in silly voices. You can even assign a voice for the day, such as reading the passage like a monster, older person, pirate, etc.
- Students can buddy read the passage, taking turns being the "reader" and the "listener," and then offering feedback to their partners.
- Read the passage as a choral reading with the entire class.

Tracking Fluency

Have students use the reproducible on page 6 to track their progress and develop goals for improving their fluency. This page can be used quarterly, weekly, or biweekly. Have students request feedback from their peers when they use the reproducible with buddy reading.

Name _____

Date _____

Reading Fluency Evaluation

	What I think			What my peer thinks		
Accuracy Did I read the words correctly?	🙂	😐	🙁	🙂	😐	🙁
Rate Was my reading just right, not too slow and not too fast?	🙂	😐	🙁	🙂	😐	🙁
Expression Did I read with feeling so that I did not sound like a robot?	🙂	😐	🙁	🙂	😐	🙁
Phrasing Did I pay attention to the punctuation marks as I read?	🙂	😐	🙁	🙂	😐	🙁

A Goal I Will Try to Meet Next Time

_____ I will read more slowly.

_____ I will read faster.

_____ I will use more expression.

_____ I will consider the punctuation.

Standards Alignment Chart

State Standards*		Weeks
Reading Standards for Literature		
Key Ideas and Details	5.RL.1–5.RL.3	1–40
Craft and Structure	5.RL.4–5.RL.6	1–7, 9, 11–19, 21–29, 31–34, 36, 38–40
Integration of Knowledge and Ideas	5.RL.7, 5.RL.9	8, 10, 14, 16, 23, 26, 31, 32, 38
Range of Reading and Level of Text Complexity	5.RL.10	1–40
Reading Standards for Informational Text		
Key Ideas and Details	5.RI.1–5.RI.3	1–40
Craft and Structure	5.RI.4–5.RI.6	1–7, 9, 11–19, 21–29, 31, 34, 36, 38, 40
Integration of Knowledge and Ideas	5.RI.7–5.RI.9	1–3, 5, 7, 9, 13–15, 20, 25, 27, 29, 31, 33, 39, 40
Range of Reading and Level of Text Complexity	5.RI.10	1–40
Writing Standards		
Each week includes a journal writing prompt to cover writing standards.		
Reading Standards: Foundational Skills		
Phonics, Word Recognition, and Fluency	5.RF.3–5.RF.4	1–40
Language Standards		
Conventions of Standard English	5.L.1–5.L.2	1–40
Knowledge of Language	5.L.3	23–29, 38
Vocabulary Acquisition and Use	5.L.4–5.L.6	1–40

The research is clear that family involvement is strongly linked to student success. Support for student learning at home improves student achievement in school. Educators should not underestimate the significance of this connection.

The fluency activities in this book create an opportunity to create or improve this school-to-home link. Students are encouraged to read their fluency passage or sight words at home with their families each week. Parents and guardians can use the reproducible tracking sheet (below) to record how their student performed in their fluency activities during the week. Students should be encouraged to return their tracking sheets to the teacher at the end of the week.

In order to make the school-to-home program work for students and their families, it may be helpful to reach out to them with an introductory letter. Explain the program and its intent and ask them to partner with you in their children's educational process. Describe the role you expect them to play. Encourage them to offer suggestions or feedback along the way.

 Fluency at Home   Name _____

- **Get Ready**—Get the passage (or sight words) for the week. Set a timer for one minute.

- **Get Set**—Start the timer when your student starts reading.

- **Go!** Mark any misread words. Record the total number of words your student read.

Week Number	1st reading words per minute	2nd reading words per minute	3rd reading words per minute	4th reading words per minute
	_____ /wpm	_____ /wpm	_____ /wpm	_____ /wpm
Problem words or phrases				

      CD-104981 • © Carson-Dellosa

Fluency Blast

Read the passage.

Juan likes baking bread and making soup. When he was just a little boy, his mom used to let him bake with her. She would give him the measuring cups and spoons and have him measure out the dry ingredients. He would need some help stirring and kneading the dough, but when it came out of the oven he was happy. He still loves the smell of fresh bread! ○○○○

Day 1

How are Australia and the United States alike and different? Australia is in the Southern Hemisphere and its summer months are December through February. The United States is in the Northern Hemisphere and its summer months are June through August. In Australia, people drive on the left side of the road. In the US, cars are driven on the right side of the road.

1. What is the main idea of this text?

   _____

   _____

2. When it is summer in Australia, which season is it in the United States? _____

3. In Australia people drive on the _____ side of the road.

Day 2

Correct the errors in each sentence.

1. Today, dad and i are going to the Park.

2. Its the Great Junkyard Race car Day!

3. The fifth graders race cars had to be built using junk.

4. I can't weight to see whose racing first!

5. the first group to race will be benjamin's Group.

Day 3

Write one synonym for each word.

1. clever _____

2. reply _____

3. wreck _____

4. applaud _____

5. shocked _____

6. angry _____

7. tired _____

8. fast _____

9. large _____

10. walk _____

Day 4

I'm a very forgetful person, so it didn't surprise any of my friends when I shouted, "I've lost my science report!" My friends all gave suggestions as to possible locations of the report, but one by one, they were **eliminated**. I hadn't stopped at my locker, the girls' gym, the computer lab, or the cafeteria.

1. Which point of view is this written from?

   A. first person   B. second person

            C. third person

2. What does **eliminated** mean?

   _____

3. Is the narrator a girl or a boy? _____

   Underline the words in the text that tell you.

1. Correct the errors in each sentence.

   My favorite teacher, Ms. Taylor, was their to.

   Oh, no! The cars wheels fell off. Thats to bad.

   Wich car is you're favorite?

2. Rewrite each sentence, replacing the words in bold with synonyms.
   A **small rabbit** was **jumping** over the **pretty** flowers.

   _____

   _____

   The **nice** boy **ran** across the **street** to get his **buddy**.

   _____

   _____

3. Reread the text on Day 1. Which text structure did the author use?

   _____

   Why was this a good way to organize the information?

   _____

   _____

Write a letter to a friend about your first week of school.

_____

_____

_____

_____

_____

_____

_____

_____

Fluency Blast

Read the passage.

Avery loves running. Her dad is a long-distance runner and used to take her with him in the stroller when he ran. As she got older, he worked to help her go longer distances. He runs marathons and Avery is working towards a half-marathon. When she gets to middle school, she wants to join the running team. Her dad said she is starting to run very fast. ○○○○

Day 1

Australia's population is about 24 million. Australia is the 53rd largest country in the world, while the United States is ranked third in world population with over 323 million people. Australia has kangaroos, anteaters, emus, and koalas, but in the United States, you'll find those animals only in zoos.

1. Which country's population is larger?

   _____

2. How does the author support this fact?

   _____

   _____

3. If an Australian was visiting the United States, where might he go to see a kangaroo?

   _____

Day 2

Correct the errors in each sentence.

1. Wow, Mrs. xun's Kindergarten class is at the race too.

2. Is that you're sister over they're?

3. it looks like theyre making repairs to the cars front end.

4. That's becuz the car is going to fall a part.

5. did you see mr. dolby's red car in the race?

Day 3

Write one antonym for each word.

1. destroy _____

2. narrow _____

3. happy _____

4. slow _____

5. huge _____

6. borrow _____

7. excited _____

8. tiny _____

9. dark _____

10. interesting _____

Day 4

Mom was upset that I'd lost my report, especially because she had been the one driving me all over town to buy just the right shade of blue printer paper. She had also done me a favor by typing the 10-page report. "Laura! How could you possibly **misplace** something so important? Did you check your backpack? Your locker?" Then, she repeated my friends' suggestions.

1. What does **misplace** mean?

   _____

2. Which word in this paragraph is a synonym for **ideas**? _____

3. Why was Laura's mom so upset?

   _____

1. Correct the errors in each sentence.

   Its the fastest car in the race.

   Im going to build the fastest car for next years race.

   Mom was pleazed and surprized that my sister's car stayed in one peace.

2. Rewrite each sentence, replacing the words in bold with antonyms.
   I **crawl** out of bed most mornings because I **hate** school.

   _____

   _____

   Mom is a **great** cook, so we **always** eat at home.

   _____

   _____

3. Reread the text on Day 4. How would you describe Laura? Support your answer.

   _____

   _____

   How would you describe Laura's mom? Support your answer.

   _____

   _____

Write about a time when you lost something.

_____

_____

_____

_____

_____

_____

_____

_____

_____

_____

Fluency Blast

Read the passage.

One of my favorite things to do is read. If my parents allowed it, I would spend the entire day with my nose in a book. I love reading about animals and planets, but the most interesting of all is a good mystery. I spend the entire book trying to figure out what is going to happen. My teacher says that I should be a detective when I grow up. Who knows, maybe I will!

OOOO

Day 1

The **official head** of Australia's government is the Queen of England. In the United States, it is the president. Australians elect people to a legislature, just like the United States. In Australia, a prime minister is the functional head of the government. An Australian law says that people who are able to vote must vote. If not, they can be fined. The United States has no such law.

1. What is the main idea of this text?

   _____

   _____

2. What does the author mean by the phrase **official head**?

   _____

Day 2

Use proofreading marks to fix the mistakes.

I wanted to tell you about buster. Hes my knew puppy! Busters fur is black and his ears are pointed. Hes always sniffing around. He likes chasing ducks at the Pond. They get so mad at him! Buster wants to play all the time, and he loves being out side. Right now, dad is giving buster a bath in tomato juice. Thats what we had to use becuz he surprized a skunk in our yard. Mom says the juice will take out the skunk smell. I shur hope so!

Day 3

Read each sentence below. If the underlined words are synonyms, write **S**. If they are antonyms, write **A**.

1. _____ Do you know if the house at the end of the street is vacant or occupied?

2. _____ Although Benji is shy now, I don't expect that he'll be timid his whole life.

3. _____ The hero of the story was courageous, and he was rewarded for being so brave.

4. _____ The plane departs at 11:00 and arrives at its destination at 2:30.

5. _____ Do you store your summer clothes in the attic or the basement?

Day 4

I had one period left before science class and I was pretty nervous because I had lost my report. I needed another A in science so that I would have straight A's across the sheet. This report was a major part of our final grade in Mrs. Garcia's class. As I sat in geography, mentally retracing my steps and **combing my memory** for ideas on the report's location, I had a great idea!

1. Do you think she will remember anything from geography class? Why or why not? _____

   _____

2. What is meant by the phrase **combing my memory**? _____

   _____

1. Use proofreading marks to fix the mistakes.

   please right and tell me what your doing.

   I can barely weight for your visit Here next month!

   Grandma and Grandpa want me too go to There house.

2. Read each sentence below. If the underlined words are synonyms, write **S**. If they are antonyms, write **A**.

   _____ The <u>presents</u> are on the table, and the guests can't wait for you to open your <u>gifts</u>.

   _____ That bread is <u>stale</u>, but I did make some <u>fresh</u> bread this morning.

   _____ Did Rascal <u>eat</u> the entire bone, or did he <u>consume</u> only part of it?

3. Complete the Venn diagram with what you know about Australia and the United States.

   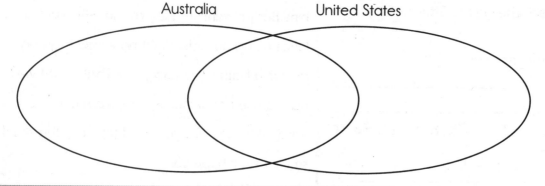
   Australia   United States

 Write at least three goals you have for yourself this year.

_____

_____

_____

_____

_____

_____

_____

_____

_____

_____

Fluency Blast

Read the passage.

Over the summer my family went to the beach. We spent a lot of time playing in the surf and building sandcastles. My little brother had me lie down, and he buried me in the sand so that the only thing you could see was my head. People walking by would look at us and chuckle. In the evening, we would eat dinner and fly kites. It was the best vacation we've ever had! ○○○○

Day 1

Marsupials and monotremes are both mammals that can be found in Australia. Marsupials carry their babies in pouches. Monotremes give birth to their young by laying eggs. However, they produce milk to feed their babies. The Tasmanian devil is a **ferocious** marsupial that lives on the island of Tasmania. It has black fur and very sharp teeth. It eats other mammals, birds, and reptiles.

1. How are marsupials and monotremes alike?

   _____

   _____

2. How are they different? _____

   _____

Day 2

Circle the choice that shows the correct capitalization.

1. tuesday, January 22
   Tuesday, January 22

2. Our Teacher is Mr. Ryan.
   Our teacher is Mr. Ryan.

3. *The house on the Hill*
   The House on the Hill

4. Police Chief Norman Lewis
   police chief Norman Lewis

5. Jamestown Elementary School
   Jamestown elementary school

Day 3

Circle the correct homophone.

1. Are you (allowed/aloud) to go to the midnight movie?

2. Practice saying your multiplication tables (allowed/aloud).

3. Caden (threw/through) the football to me.

4. The tunnel goes (threw/through) the mountain.

5. I asked (to/two/too) friends (to/two/too) come over because I was (to/two/too) bored.

Day 4

Neil was not very good at math, and his grades were not **spectacular**. However, he was determined to work hard. He began studying with his two older sisters every night. After a few weeks, his grades really improved. Much to his teacher's surprise, Neil received an A on the year's final test. With his sisters' help and his parents' encouragement, he is now a much better student.

1. What does **spectacular** mean?

   _____

2. What caused Neil's grades to improve?

   _____

3. How would you describe Neil's family?

   _____

1. Underline with three short lines the first letter of words that need to be capitalized.

   did the movie *around the world in 80 days* win an academy award in 1956?

   does grandpa get the chicago sun-times or the chicago tribune?

   we're going to an italian restaurant on friday night after we read *strega nona*.

2. Read each sentence. Circle the letter of the correct definition for the underlined homophone.

   Denise will have many books to <u>buy</u> when she starts college.

   A. to purchase   B. to be near

   The horse's <u>mane</u> glistened in the morning sunshine.

   A. the most important   B. hair

3. Reread the text on Day 1. What kind of animal is the Tasmanian devil?

   _____

   What is the meaning of **ferocious**?

   _____

   How does the author support the idea that the Tasmanian devil is ferocious?

   _____

Think about the kind of student you are. Using the word *student*, write an acrostic poem describing yourself.

_____

_____

_____

_____

_____

_____

_____

_____

_____

Fluency Blast

Read the passage.

My friend's birthday is today and her parents are throwing her a surprise party. In order for it to remain a surprise, we have to arrive early. Heath and Grey are bringing board games as presents. Jan got her a purple knit sweater. I bought her a poster of her favorite musical artist. I hope that she is excited when she walks in and sees us! ○○○○

Day 1

The duck-billed platypus is classified as a monotreme because it is an egg-laying mammal but still produces milk to feed her young. It has soft fur, a snout, webbed feet and claws, and a flat tail like a beaver. It lives near rivers and creeks, where it eats crawfish, worms, and small fish. The platypus uses its **unique** bill to find and catch prey underwater.

1. Why do you think a duck-billed platypus lives near rivers and creeks? _____

2. Describe how a duck-billed platypus looks.
   _____
   _____

3. What does **unique** mean?_____
   _____

Day 2

Circle the correct spelling of each plural noun.

1. I made a lot of (friendes/friends).

2. Two (foxes/foxs) ran by camp today.

3. We won't get too close to the (cliffs/clives).

4. The (leaves/leafs) are turning colors.

5. I found a pretty leaf that is the color of (cherrys/cherries).

6. I have to practice for the (playes/plays) now.

Day 3

Circle the correct homophone.

1. The mama (bare/bear) protected her cubs.

2. The cupboard was (bare/bear).

3. She was so hungry she (ate/eight) an entire pizza.

4. My little brother is (ate/eight) years old.

5. I (knew/new) my dad was getting (knew/new) shoes.

Day 4

Dear Paige,
   How are you? Are you getting excited for summer? I am going to volunteer at the local animal shelter. What are your plans? Will you be camping with your parents again? That would be so much fun! Well, I need to get back to reading about animal care. Write back soon!
Your friend, Quiana

1. Why do you think Quiana is reading about animal care?
   _____
   _____

2. What point of view is this letter told from?
   A. first person   B. second person
              C. third person

1. Circle the correct spelling.

   I have visited many different (cityes/cities) in the past year.

   My mother always loses her (keys/keyes).

   I love listening to the (birdes/birds) sing in the morning.

2. Read each sentence. Circle the letter of the correct definition for the underlined homophone.
   Ebony lives <u>by</u> the pond with the ducks and geese.
   A. to purchase   B. to be near

   Please underline the sentence with the <u>main</u> idea in this paragraph.
   A. the most important   B. hair

3. Reread the text on Day 1. What kind of animal is the duck-billed platypus?
   A. marsupial   B. monotreme

   Write a title for the text.

   _____

Write a letter to a friend telling them about your favorite parts of your summer.

_____

_____

_____

_____

_____

_____

_____

_____

Fluency Blast

Read the passage.

Sundays are lazy days at our house. We get up a little later and make breakfast together as a family. Our favorite meal is pancakes and bacon. After breakfast, we work on the crossword puzzle. Sometimes we go to the park and other times we watch a movie. We always order pizza and play board games at night. It is such a fun way to end the weekend! ○ ○ ○ ○

Day 1

The Sydney Opera House is world famous. It is one of the most unusual buildings in the world. The opera house is in Sydney and is Australia's most famous **landmark**. It is located in Sydney Harbor. The opera house contains one hall for operas. The orchestra plays in another hall. A third hall is for plays. A fourth is for chamber music. The fifth is for exhibitions.

1. Do you think the opera house is near water?

   _____

2. Underline the detail from the text that supports your answer.

3. What is a **landmark**?

   _____

   _____

Day 2

Write the plural form of each noun.

1. boss _____

2. country _____

3. boy _____

4. roof _____

5. calf _____

6. tax _____

7. fly _____

8. donkey _____

9. chief _____

10. wife _____

Day 3

Read each sentence. Then, choose the sentence in which the underlined word is used the same way as it is in the first sentence.

1. Mom says that Felicia has a <u>mind</u> for numbers.

   A. Do you <u>mind</u> if I try your dessert?

   B. A <u>mind</u> is a terrible thing to waste.

2. Gabe earned extra points for good <u>conduct</u>.

   A. It takes years to learn how to <u>conduct</u> an orchestra.

   B. Hayden's <u>conduct</u> at the performance made his parents proud.

Day 4

They call me a three-toed sloth, but
   everyone knows,
When you count them all up, I have
   12 gorgeous toes.
I require splendid, tropical rain forests in
   order to **survive**,
For if it weren't for them, I most certainly
   wouldn't be alive.

1. What genre of writing is this? _____

2. How do you know?

   _____

3. What does **survive** mean?

   _____

1. Write the plural form of each noun.

carrot _____   knife _____   wish _____

waltz _____   church _____   worry _____

spider _____   cup _____   page _____

2. Write two sentences using the homograph **bat**. Be sure each sentence shows a different meaning.

_____

_____

_____

_____

3. Reread the text on Day 4. How many legs do you think the sloth has?

_____

What evidence from the text supports your answer?

_____

_____

Write a title for the text.

_____

Write an acrostic poem about a sloth.

_____

_____

_____

_____

_____

_____

_____

_____

Fluency Blast

Read the passage.

Jayla has come over for dinner every night this week. Her parents are out of town and her older brother is staying with her. She says he is a horrible cook and begged my mom to eat with us. Of course, my mom said she could since she is my best friend. We work on homework and watch a little television before her brother picks her up. I think next week will be pretty boring. ○○○○

Day 1

Danish architect Jørn Utzon designed the Sydney Opera House. Work began in 1959 and was completed in 1973. The estimate for the project was $7 million (Australian). However, the final cost was $102 million. Utzon wanted the roof to look like sails on a giant sailing ship. The roof is made of 10 gigantic arched-concrete shell shapes. Working on the building was dangerous because of the roof.

1. How long did it take to build the Sydney Opera House? _____

2. What was the final cost of the building?

   _____

3. Describe the roof of the building. _____

   _____

Day 2

Write the plural form of each noun.

1. child _____
2. tooth _____
3. cactus _____
4. foot _____
5. ox _____
6. fish _____
7. mouse _____
8. woman _____
9. deer _____
10. potato _____

Day 3

Read each sentence. Then, choose the sentence in which the underlined word is used the same way as it is in the first sentence.

1. "I object, Your Honor!" shouted the attorney.

   A. If you don't object to eating late, we'll have dinner at 8:00.

   B. The object of the game is to get rid of all your cards.

2. I'd like you to take the lead during Monday's presentation.

   A. Paint in old houses sometimes contains lead.

   B. "Once we're on the trail," said Audrey, "you take the lead."

Day 4

Rachel and Shane are **swaying** slowly in the family swing. The air is crisp and cool. Rachel puts her arm around Shane and snuggles into his shaggy body. Shane's tongue licks Rachel's hand, which lies on her blue-jean clad leg. They watch a sluggish ladybug crawl underneath a pile of old, brown leaves. One red leaf drifts down to the top of the ladybug's pile.

1. What does **swaying** mean?

   _____

2. What is Shane?

   _____

3. What time of year is it? _____

   Underline the words in the text that tell you.

1. Write the plural form of each noun.

goose _____   volcano _____   moose _____

loaf _____   sheep _____   puppy _____

man _____   person _____   dog _____

2. Write two sentences using the homograph **fine**. Be sure each sentence shows a different meaning.

_____

_____

_____

_____

3. Reread the text on Day 1. Does the Sydney Opera House look like Utzon wanted it to? Explain.

_____

_____

What details in the text support your answer?

_____

_____

Why did the author write this passage?

_____

_____

Write a short story about a dog and its owner.

_____

_____

_____

_____

_____

_____

_____

_____

_____

Fluency Blast

Read the passage.

I was sick and ran badly during the competition, but Chase had a great day and ran well. My day was horrible because I lost, but it was a fantastic day for my teammate. Chase accepted his praises well. I decided I will train harder so I could do better in my next race. Chase said that he will help me and that we can run every day after school. ○○○○

Day 1

Green plants are like factories. Plant factories make two kinds of food: sugar and starch. Almost all fruits and vegetables you eat contain some form of sugar or starch. Fruits such as apples and cherries contain sugar; vegetables such as potatoes and beans contain starch. Green plants are made of cells. Because they are so small, cells can only be seen through a microscope. Inside the cells are chloroplasts, the machines of the plant factory.

1. What does the author compare green plants with? _____

2. What two kinds of food do plant factories make? _____

3. Green plants are made of _____ .

Day 2

List at least 5 examples of abstract nouns for each category.

Feelings	Character Traits
love	bravery
_____	_____
_____	_____
_____	_____
_____	_____
_____	_____
_____	_____
_____	_____

Day 3

Read each sentence. Then, choose the sentence in which the underlined word is used the same way as it is in the first sentence.

1. Try not to <u>tear</u> the leaves when you plant the seedlings.

   A. How did you <u>tear</u> your jacket?

   B. A single <u>tear</u> dripped down Mrs. Avery's cheek.

2. Did you <u>suspect</u> that Ian planned a surprise party?

   A. The <u>suspect</u> in the robbery will be tried in court next week.

   B. I <u>suspect</u> that Jack has candy hidden in his room.

Day 4

Shane's graying ears prick up as a flock of geese honks good-bye. The sky slowly turns from blue, to pink, to purple, to black as Rachel's mom calls her in to eat. Rachel gives one last push as she slides out of the swing. She walks to the back door of the house. Shane leaps down. He barks once at a rabbit and then chases after Rachel. She smiles and rubs Shane's head as they walk into the warm house together.

1. If the author was recording this story, which sounds would contribute to the beauty of the text? _____

   _____

2. Is Shane a puppy or an older dog? _____
   Underline the words in the text that tell you.

1. Look back at Day 2. Write three sentences containing words from your lists.

_____
_____
_____
_____
_____

2. Write two sentences using the homograph **lead**. Be sure each sentence shows a different meaning.

_____
_____

_____
_____

3. Reread the text on Day 4. How do you think Rachel feels? _____
   List the words in the story that give a picture of laziness.

_____
_____

   Write a title for the story.

_____

Write about a lazy time you have had.

_____
_____
_____
_____
_____
_____
_____
_____
_____

Fluency Blast

Read the passage.

My sister is much older than I am, and she recently had a baby girl. I was beyond excited to find out that I am an aunt! I am already spending lots of time with my niece. She is extremely adorable. Her name is Emma, and she has an entire head of dark hair and the tiniest fingers I have ever seen. In the beginning, I was afraid to hold her, but now I am used to it! ○○○○

Day 1

Stomata are tiny holes in leaves that allow air to move in and out. Plants use carbon dioxide and then release oxygen back into the air. Roots allow water to travel in through the root hairs. Plants use storerooms to **store** their food. Carrots store their food in roots, while maple trees store their food in trunks. Lettuce plants store their food in leaves, peas store their food in seeds, and peach trees store their food in the fruit.

1. What is the meaning of **store**? _____
   _____

2. Where do carrots store food? _____

3. Circle the main topic of this paragraph.

Day 2

Read each noun. If it is abstract, write **A**. If it is concrete, write **C**.

1. _____ joy
2. _____ freedom
3. _____ school
4. _____ beauty
5. _____ puppy
6. _____ carrot
7. _____ anger
8. _____ strength
9. _____ baseball
10. _____ mom
11. _____ trust
12. _____ smart

Day 3

Read each sentence. Write **S** if it contains a simile and **M** if it contains a metaphor. Then, write the two things being compared.

1. _____ Garrett slept as soundly as a bear in winter.
   _____ compared to _____

2. _____ The grass was a cool carpet beneath Iesha's feet.
   _____ compared to _____

3. _____ Aunt Heather was a mama bear when it came to protecting her children.
   _____ compared to _____

Day 4

"Hey, Mom!" hollered Spencer. "Guess what I learned about in school today." He found a picture in a magazine and showed it to her. "Oh, my, what is that?" exclaimed his mom. "A hairy-nosed wombat. It's a type of wombat that lives in burrows underground. Their habitats are **declining**, and they are endangered. They have soft, gray fur, even on their noses. Unfortunately, they are not pets." "Well, I'm glad to hear that," laughed Mom.

1. What does **declining** mean?
   _____

2. How does Spencer feel about hairy-nosed wombats? _____

Underline the words in the text that tell you.

1. What makes a noun concrete?

_____

What makes a noun abstract?

_____

2. Reread Day 3. Choose two of the sentences. Explain what each simile or metaphor means.

_____

_____

3. Reread the text on Day 1. How is the text organized?

_____

List three facts about green plants.

_____

_____

_____

_____

Write a compare-and-contrast paragraph about how living in the city is different from or the same as living in the country.

_____

_____

_____

_____

_____

_____

_____

_____

Fluency Blast

Read the passage.

My grandparents took me to a basketball game last weekend. I play basketball with my neighbors frequently and have always wanted to go to a game. We sat right down at center court where I could see all of the action. The spectators clapped and cheered loudly throughout the game. I participated, and by the end of the game, I could barely talk.

○○○○

Day 1

Television is a window allowing you to see other people, places, and events around the world. More than 97 percent of all US homes have a television. How does a television work? First, light and sound waves are changed into electronic signals by cameras and microphones. Next, these signals are passed through the air and received by individual television sets. Last, the television set unscrambles the signals.

1. To what does the author compare a television to? _____

2. Why did the author write this text? _____
   _____

3. How do you feel about television? _____
   _____

Day 2

Read the sentences. If they have incorrect subject/verb agreement, correct the verb.

1. Sally and I am going to the park.

2. The basket of books are on the table.

3. Neither Tara nor Uma is studying today.

4. There is three tests next week.

5. She is going with me to shop.

Day 3

Read each sentence. Write **S** if it contains a simile and **M** if it contains a metaphor. Then, write the two things being compared.

1. _____ The full moon was a plump, friendly face peeking over the hill.
   _____ compared to _____

2. _____ In the middle of rush hour, the highway was a parking lot.
   _____ compared to _____

3. _____ Jacob was excited to go, but his brother moved as slowly as molasses.
   _____ compared to _____

Day 4

A crow was about to enjoy a tasty treat she had found. A fox wandered by and said, "How lovely you look! I bet your voice is just as beautiful." The crow puffed up her feathers and opened her beak to sing. As she did this, the treat fell out of her mouth and tumbled to the ground. The fox grabbed it and devoured it. He smiled slyly, calling out, "It is not wise to trust those who praise you with many compliments."

1. Why do you think the fox said nice things to the crow? _____
   _____

2. Do you think the fox meant those compliments? Why? _____
   _____

1. Circle the correct verb.

   Everyone (need/needs) to study for the spelling test.

   Victor and Vanessa (give/gives) their little brother hugs.

   Either my aunt or my uncle (is/are) taking me to the game.

2. Reread Day 3. Choose one of the sentences. Explain what the simile or metaphor means.

   _____

   _____

3. Reread the text on Day 4. What is the theme of the story?

   _____

   _____

   What visual could you add to the text to contribute to its meaning?

   _____

   _____

Write about a time you have complimented someone to get what you wanted.

_____

_____

_____

_____

_____

_____

_____

_____

Fluency Blast

Read the passage.

Gavin learned to play the guitar because he wanted to start his own band. Many of his friends play instruments, and they have been working hard to learn new songs. Grace pounds her drums, and Dion strums his electric bass. They get to play a show in front of an audience next week, and they are very nervous. I have told them many times that they should not worry. ○○○○

Day 1

Television has more than one inventor. In the 1800s, G. Marconi **set the stage** when he discovered how to send signals through the air as electromagnetic waves. His invention was the radio. In the early 1900s, P. Farnsworth thought to send pictures as well as sound. This led to the electronic television camera. Then, V. Zworykin invented a television camera and a picture tube to receive and show the picture. In 1929, he made the first television system.

1. What is the meaning of the phrase **set the stage**? _____

2. Who invented the radio?_____

When did Zworykin make the first TV system? _____

Day 2

Use a present- or past-tense verb to complete each sentence.

1. Xander _____ a good question in science class earlier.

2. As they look at the pictures, the ladies _____ at its beauty.

3. I _____ at the stars as I walk outside.

4. Yasmin and Peter, please _____ that in your report.

5. Zach and Porchia _____ when they are late.

Day 3

Read each sentence. Write **S** if it contains a simile and **M** if it contains a metaphor. Then, write the two things being compared.

1. _____Kenyon is a night owl—he rarely goes to bed before midnight.

_____ compared to _____

2. _____The wildflowers were as colorful as confetti thrown into the air.

_____ compared to _____

3. _____The moon was a misty shadow because of the clouds.

_____ compared to _____

Day 4

Dear Lola,

I have some sad news. On Monday, our favorite restaurant burned down. I saw the huge, thick, black cloud of smoke. Kennedy was with me, and she was crying, "I want to go home!" She was as scared as a turkey on Thanksgiving. The owners must be so upset. I think I will write them a card.

Write soon, Brianna

1. Underline the simile. What does it mean?

_____

2. What type of text is this?

_____

3. Who do you think Kennedy is?

_____

1. Use a present- or past-tense verb to complete each sentence.

   The crowd _____ and cheered many times during the game.

   Abe fell on the ice. But, he _____ about it later.

   Benjamin _____ waffles for breakfast.

2. Reread Day 3. Choose one of the sentences. Explain what the simile or metaphor means.

   _____

   _____

3. Reread the text on Day 1. How did the author organize the text?

   _____

   About how much time passed from the invention of the radio to the television?

   _____

   Do you think Farnsworth or Zworykin made a lot of money from their invention of the television? Why or why not?

   _____

   _____

✏️ **Write about your favorite television show.**

_____

_____

_____

_____

_____

_____

_____

_____

Fluency Blast

Read the passage.

Do you believe in haunted houses? How about haunted hotels? Ohio is home to the Buxton Inn and people believe it is haunted. The hotel was built in 1812, and in the 1920s one ghost was seen in the kitchen eating a piece of pie. Many guests have seen a ghost in the dining room. Some people have even seen a kitty roaming throughout the inn. It has been named Major Buxton. ○○○○

Day 1

Philo Farnsworth was born in a log cabin in 1906. When he was 12, he moved to a ranch. Farnsworth was miles away from a school, so he rode a horse to get there. He was curious about electrons and electricity. He asked a teacher to tutor him and to let him sit in on a course for older students. The teacher agreed. When he was 14, he came up with the idea of sending television pictures without using moving parts.

1. What is the main idea of this text? _____
_____

2. How would you describe Philo Farnsworth?
_____

3. Underline the words in the text that suppport your answer.

Day 2

Underline the progressive verb phrase in each sentence.

1. We are walking to school every day this week.

2. She was going to clean her room last night.

3. Bill and Cameron will be watching a movie tonight.

4. Drew was sleeping when the fire alarm sounded.

5. I am taking a spelling test today.

Day 3

Write one simile or metaphor to describe each item.

1. the freshly fallen snow
_____
_____

2. the crowd in the stadium
_____
_____

3. the sand on the beach
_____
_____

Day 4

1. What type of text feature is this?
_____

2. Is this text organized thematically or chronologically? _____
_____

3. What season is it in chapters 1 and 2? _____
How do you know? _____
_____

1. Write two sentences that contain a progressive verb phrase.

_____

_____

_____

_____

2. Write one simile and one metaphor about school.

_____

_____

_____

_____

3. Reread the text on Day 4. What do you think the author wrote about in chapter 4?

_____

_____

If the author added two more chapters, what might the titles be?

_____

_____

Reread the text on Day 1. Write a letter to Philo Farnsworth. Explain what you think about television and ask him at least one question.

_____

_____

_____

_____

_____

_____

_____

_____

_____

Fluency Blast

Read the passage.

Firefighting is a brave and courageous job. If you can't imagine yourself working hard, then this job isn't for you. Firefighters must go through special training. They don't ever take training lightly. They must wear special gear and use special equipment. It isn't easy to use the equipment. Firefighters must train in actual fires.

○○○○

Day 1

Philo Farnsworth invented the television. How did it work? Moving images were broken into pinpoints of light. These were changed into electrical impulses, or movements. Then, the impulses were collected in the television set and changed back into light. People could then see the images. When he died in 1971, Farnsworth held over 300 patents for inventions. A major magazine listed him as one of the 100 greatest scientists and thinkers of the twentieth century.

1. What is the main idea of this text?

   _____

2. Farnsworth is considered a great scientist and thinker. How does the author support this?

   _____

Day 2

Read each sentence. If the progressive verb is present tense, write **PR**. If it is past tense, write **P**. If it is future tense, write **F**.

1. _____ Ella lost her bracelet when she was running.

2. _____ I am walking home after school.

3. _____ We will be going to the movies tonight.

4. _____ You are being silly right now!

5. _____ They were helping Mom clean the house.

Day 3

Write one simile and one metaphor to describe each item.

1. the nervous girl

   _____

   _____

   _____

2. the fuzzy puppy

   _____

   _____

   _____

Day 4

A mighty oak tree grew along a riverbank. Its trunk was thick, and its branches reached high. It **towered proudly** above a patch of reeds growing below. When a breeze blew across the river, the leaves of the oak danced, but its branches held on firmly. The oak laughed at the reeds because they trembled and shook as they struggled to stand up straight. The reeds did not mind the laughter of the oak; after all, the tree was so much bigger and stronger.

1. How does the oak feel about the reeds?

   _____

2. What does **towered proudly** mean?

   _____

1. Write one sentence with a past progressive verb phrase and one sentence with a future progressive verb phrase.

   _____

   _____

   _____

   _____

2. Write one simile and one metaphor about your family.

   _____

   _____

   _____

   _____

3. Think about what you know about Philo Farnsworth. What do you think led Farnsworth to invent the television?

   _____

   _____

   _____

4. Reread the text on Day 4. Write a title for it.

   _____

Describe an experience you've had or a trip you've taken. Use at least two similes and two metaphors.

_____

_____

_____

_____

_____

_____

_____

_____

Fluency Blast

Read the passage.

Some people that train to be firefighters don't make it completely through training. They may find out they don't like climbing ladders that are so high, or they aren't strong enough. The firefighters who graduate are ready for the job. They never know what dangers each day will bring, but they are trained and ready. Firefighters keep our homes safe. ○○○○

Day 1

While your hair may improve your appearance, it has important functions. It acts as a cushion, protecting the head. It can be a shield from the hot summer sun and keep the head warm on chilly days. Inside the nose and ears, tiny hairs deter dirt, dust, and insects from entering the body. Eyebrows trap perspiration before it is able to reach the eyes. Eyelashes prevent dirt and dust from infecting the eyes.

1. How does the author feel about hair?

   _____

2. How does the author support this opinion?

   _____

   _____

Day 2

Circle the best modal verb to complete each sentence.

1. You (could/should) always tell the truth.

2. We (may/must) arrive on time or else we will be in trouble.

3. (Will/May) you please tell me the time?

4. We (should/might) prepare for the final exam.

5. I (will/might) find my socks anywhere.

Day 3

Write the meaning of each idiom or proverb.

1. a heart of gold

   _____

2. a watched pot never boils

   _____

3. a picture is worth a thousand words

   _____

4. a drop in the bucket

   _____

5. that slipped my mind

   _____

Day 4

One day, a terrible hurricane approached a river. Its violent winds pulled up the roots of a mighty oak and tossed it to the ground. The great tree lay in a patch of reeds. The oak spoke sadly, "The strong winds threw me to the ground like a stick. Yet you reeds were able to stay rooted even though you are much smaller." One reed spoke, "We may be small, but we know how to bend. You, mighty oak, were too proud and did not know how to bend."

1. What caused the oak tree to fall? _____

   _____

2. What character trait did the mighty oak show? _____ How did this affect him?

   _____

1. Write two sentences that contain modal verbs. Switch with a partner and underline the modal verb phrases.

   _____

   _____

   _____

2. Reread Day 3. Pick two idioms/proverbs and use each in a complete sentence.

   _____

   _____

   _____

   _____

3. Reread the text on Day 4. What is the lesson in the text?

   _____

   How might a nonfiction article describe the differences between an oak tree and reeds differently?

   _____

   _____

   _____

   _____

   _____

   _____

Write about the character trait that you show the most. Give examples of this trait in your life.

   _____

   _____

   _____

   _____

   _____

   _____

   _____

   _____

Fluency Blast

Read the passage.

As I slowly wandered toward the science lab, I thought about what I would tell my teacher. I had misplaced my report. I silently rehearsed some excuses. I began to feel guilty and wondered if I could look my favorite teacher in the eye and lie about my report. How would I feel then? Maybe I would feel more horrible than I felt when I realized the report was missing. ○○○○

Day 1

Each hair on the body grows from a root beneath the skin. This root forms a tiny tube called a **follicle**. As new hair cells grow from the root, the old cells are pushed up. They soon die because they are no longer being fed. The dead cells harden, forming a stack on top of a root, referred to as a hair shaft. It is the hair we see. Only the follicle and the root remain alive.

1. What is a hair shaft made of?

   _____

2. What are the three parts of each hair strand?

   _____

   _____

   _____

Day 2

Read each sentence. If the underlined verb is past perfect, write **PP**. If it is present perfect, write **PR**. If it is future perfect, write **FP**.

1. _____ Soon, I <u>will have finished</u> reading this book.

2. _____ I <u>have enjoyed</u> the first several chapters.

3. _____ Until now, I <u>had not read</u> any other books by the author.

4. _____ I <u>have been reading</u> nonstop all week.

5. _____ By next summer, I <u>will have read</u> all of her books.

Day 3

Write the meaning of each idiom or proverb.

1. don't put all of your eggs in one basket

   _____

2. it cost an arm and a leg

   _____

3. a penny saved is a penny earned

   _____

4. get your act together

   _____

5. a change of heart

   _____

Day 4

I love water sports, especially waterskiing. That's why I invited my best friend, Raul, over to give it a try. Raul had never been on water skis before, but he was a good athlete. So, I thought waterskiing would be a **breeze** for him. Waterskiing is like flying to me. When I am being pulled on water skis behind the boat, I feel like an eagle in flight. However, I soon realized Raul was more of an albatross than an eagle.

1. What is the meaning of **breeze** in this text?

   _____

2. How is Raul at waterskiing?

   _____

   _____

Underline the words in the text that tell you.

1. Write one sentence with a past perfect tense verb phrase and one with a future perfect verb phrase.

   _____

   _____

   _____

   _____

2. Reread Day 3. Choose one idiom/proverb and use it in a complete sentence.

   _____

   _____

3. Reread the text on Day 1. What text feature could add to a reader's understanding? Create it in the space provided.

   _____

Tell about a time you did not have your homework.

_____

_____

_____

_____

_____

_____

_____

_____

CD-104981 • © Carson-Dellosa

Fluency Blast

Read the passage.

I tossed my backpack over my shoulder, straightened my back, and wandered into the science lab. Taking a deep breath, I knew what I needed to do—I needed to tell the truth. I walked up to Mrs. Edwards' desk in order to speak with her. As she looked up from the thick stack of papers in front of her, she lightly tapped the top report.

○ ○ ○ ○

Day 1

The shape of the hair shaft, as seen under a microscope, determines the degree of curliness or straightness. Straight hairs are round in structure. The flatter the hair shaft, the curlier the hair will be. You cannot change your hair follicles, but hair straighteners and perms can alter the appearance of hair temporarily.

1. What is the main idea of this text?

   _____

2. Can you change the shape of your hair? Explain. _____

   _____

3. What shape is your hair shaft? _____

   _____

Day 2

Underline the perfect tense phrase in each sentence.

1. I have watched backyard birds for many years.

2. I had noticed that my yard was very quiet during the winter.

3. The birds had gone elsewhere to find food.

4. I have been excited to see who comes to visit me now.

5. I have been adding new feeders to my yard every year.

Day 3

Read each idiom. Write the letter of the meaning.

1. _____ at a snail's pace
2. _____ to jump the gun
3. _____ down the drain
4. _____ couch potato
5. _____ under the weather

_____

A. to do something before it's time

B. a person who watches lots of TV or is lazy

C. to do something very slowly

D. to feel sick

E. something is lost or wasted

Day 4

I was teaching Raul to ski. On his first try, he let go of the rope as soon as the boat moved. He sank like an anchor. On his second try, he flipped head over heels like a gymnast. On his third try, Raul stood up. He teetered back and forth like a rag doll until he fell over. He held on to the rope after he lost both skis. As he flopped at the end of the rope like a fish, I realized that waterskiing is not for everyone.

1. Underline the similes. Choose one and write it.

   _____

   _____

2. What is the meaning of the simile? _____

   _____

1. Underline the perfect verb phrase in each sentence below.

   By next winter, I will have built three more wooden feeders.

   I also will have stocked each one with a different kind of bird seed.

   These tiny visitors have added a touch of color to my days.

2. Reread Day 3. Choose two idioms to use in sentences.

   _____

   _____

   _____

   _____

3. Reread the text on Day 4. What is the theme of this text?

   _____

   _____

   What other texts have you read with a similar theme?

   _____

   _____

Write a story about a time you tried something new.

_____

_____

_____

_____

_____

_____

_____

_____

_____

Fluency Blast

Read the passage.

The dragonfly and the bumblebee circled the flower. Both Henry and Blaze enjoyed spending the day flitting through the field. There were so many beautiful plants to choose from. Sometimes they landed on the same plant and it caused problems. They had been friends for a very long time and didn't mind sharing, but sometimes they wouldn't both fit on a flower.

○○○○

Day 1

Clara Brown was born a slave in 1800. She married another slave when she was 18. They had four children. In 1835, she and her family were auctioned off to different slave owners. Clara was sold to George Brown. Her husband and son were bought by slave traders. Her daughters were sold to another slave owner. Clara lost touch with all of her family. She spent many years searching for them. Finally, in 1882, she found one daughter, Eliza Jane, in Iowa.

1. How did the author organize the information in this text? _____

_____

2. How would you describe Clara's life?

_____

Day 2

Read each sentence. On the line, write the boldface verb in the past (**PP**), present (**PR**), or future (**FP**) perfect tense.

1. Fiona **volunteer** at Lakeside Waterfowl Rescue. (**PR**)

_____

2. Cadence **work** with Fiona for the last six months. (**PR**)

_____

3. They **rescue** dozens of birds every month. (**PP**)

_____

4. The rescue **provide** fresh food and water daily. (**PP**)

_____

Day 3

Read each idiom. Write the letter of the meaning.

1. _____ get the ball rolling
2. _____ a needle in a haystack
3. _____ at the 11th hour
4. _____ to tighten your belt
5. _____ all ears

A. to spend less money

B. at the last minute

C. to get things started

D. to be listening

E. hard to find

Day 4

Sanding the board, my sweet White Socks.
Her tongue, like fine grains of sand
On paper, licking the wood.
She is an electric sander
Giving out a quiet purr.
She is a nail file,
Smoothing out the edges.

1. What is White Socks?_____
2. What evidence supports your answer?

_____

_____

3. Circle the simile and underline the metaphors.

1. Read each sentence. Write the boldface verb in the past (**PP**), present (**PR**), or future (**FP**) perfect tense.

   The rescue **rely** on its volunteers to take care of the animals. (**PR**)

   _____

   At the end of the summer, Fiona **earn** an award for hours donated. (**FP**)

   _____

2. Reread Day 3. Choose two idioms to use in sentences.

   _____

   _____

   _____

   _____

3. Reread the text on Day 4. What type of text is this?

   _____

   What do you think White Socks is doing?

   _____

   _____

Write a poem about an animal.

_____

_____

_____

_____

_____

_____

_____

_____

_____

_____

Fluency Blast

Read the passage.

The Teton Mountain Range is a beautiful sight and is a challenge for rock climbers. It is located in Wyoming. Because of its beauty, more than three million people visit each year. Rock climbers come from all over the world. Many climbers say the view from the mountain is breathtaking. They also agree that wildlife viewing is amazing.

○○○○

Day 1

The 1850 census showed that about 4 million African Americans were living in the United States. Only 400,000 of these African Americans were free. Free African Americans had to obey laws **established** for them. In many states, they could not learn to read or write and were not allowed to testify in court. They could not hold meetings or preach in public places. It took many years for these laws to change.

1. What is the main idea of this text?

_____

2. What does **established** mean?

_____

3. How many African Americans were not slaves in 1850? _____

Day 2

Complete each sentence with the word in parentheses. Use the correct tense so that it agrees with the rest of the sentence.

1. My family pulled up to the cabin and _____ the car. (unload)

2. We _____ at the same cabin every year, and I love it! (stay)

3. The inside is not fancy, but it _____ homey and cozy. (is)

4. Mom unloaded the groceries, and Dad _____ a fire. (start)

5. It _____ the small cabin quickly. (warm)

Day 3

Write **S** if the sentence is a simile, **M** if it is a metaphor, **I** if it is an idiom, and **P** if it is a proverb.

1. _____ Who let the cat out of the bag?

2. _____ The Olympic jumper soared through the air like a bird.

3. _____ Don't judge a book by its cover.

4. _____ The early bird catches the worm.

5. _____ The waterfall was a laughing giant roaring over the cliff.

6. _____ Curiosity killed the cat.

7. _____ The skater was a graceful swan as she glided across the ice.

Day 4

Torika is Chinese American. Each week, her family members gather and serve a **traditional** Chinese meal. This week, Torika invited her friend Ruby to join them. When Ruby arrived, Torika directed her through the living room to the kitchen, which was filled with many good smells. Torika and Ruby set the table. They gave each person a pair of chopsticks, a soup bowl, a soup spoon, and a rice bowl on a saucer.

1. What does **traditional** mean?

_____

2. What types of food do you think will be served?

_____

_____

1. Complete each sentence below with the word in parentheses. Use the correct tense so it agrees with the rest of the sentence.

   When I was six, I _____ my hand roasting marshmallows in the fireplace. (burn)

   Next year, we will come in June, and we _____ my cousins here. (meet)

2. Use the following idioms in sentences that show their meanings.
   pig out

   _____

   _____

   cry crocodile tears

   _____

   _____

3. Reread the text on Day 1. Why do you think these specific laws were passed?

   _____

   _____

   _____

   _____

Write a letter to a famous person whom you admire.

_____

_____

_____

_____

_____

_____

_____

_____

_____

_____

Fluency Blast

Read the passage.

The ancient Cherokee were hunters and farmers. They lived in the mountain area of Georgia. But in 1829, white settlers found gold on this land. They went to the government and asked that the Cherokee be forced to leave in the hopes they would then get the rights to that land. A new law was passed in 1830 forcing the Cherokee to move.

○○○○

Day 1

Clara Brown became free in 1857. African Americans had to carry **freedom papers** at all times to prove that they were not runaway slaves. Clara took a job as a cook on a wagon train heading to Colorado. She hoped she would find her daughter there. In Colorado, Clara started a laundry business. She helped pay for ex-slaves to move to Colorado.

1. Why did Clara take a job as a cook on a wagon train? _____
_____

2. What were **freedom papers**? _____
_____
_____

Day 2

Circle and correct each incorrect shift in verb tense in the paragraph.

After college, Emily plans to join the Peace

Corps. She applies last year and was accepted.

Mom and Dad knew how important it is to her,

so they throw her a big party. It will be strange

to have my big sister go so far away, and I

know I missed her a lot. I looked forward to

hearing about all of her experiences in Africa.

Day 3

Circle the correct word.

1. He and Orlando are (hour/our) cousins.
2. My dad (lies/lays) in the hammock for hours.
3. (Affects/Effects) of the earthquake are everywhere (accept/except) the shelter.
4. Patsy has (lain/laid) her scissors on the desk.
5. The papers have (laid/lain) on the desk for weeks.
6. My library book was (dew/due) last (weak/week).
7. Did those (ate/eight) (flours/flowers) come from your yard?

Day 4

Torika and Ruby went into the kitchen. Torika's father was slicing vegetables. He threw them into a large pan coated with oil. "That's a wok," Torika explained. Ruby watched the vegetables sizzle. Ruby carried the steamed rice. It was one of the few dishes she recognized. There were wontons, steamed noodles, stir-fried beef, sweet-and-sour chicken, and spareribs. The **nutritious** food was seasoned with herbs and sauces.

1. Do you think Ruby was upset about helping?
_____

2. What does **nutritious** mean?
_____

1. Write **C** next to the sentence if it uses the correct verb tense. Write **N** if it does not.

_____ Felipe drew a picture of his cat and painted a picture of his dog.

_____ Right now, he is taking sculpture lessons and learned photography.

_____ He might be a famous artist when he grew up.

2. Use each word in a sentence to show its meaning.

(too) _____

_____

(sea) _____

_____

(whether) _____

_____

3. Reread the text on Day 4. Circle the name of the only thing Ruby was familiar with before the dinner.

      wok   chopsticks   rice   wontons

How do you think Ruby is used to eating?

_____

Use descriptive language to write about your favorite food.

_____

_____

_____

_____

_____

_____

_____

_____

_____

_____

Fluency Blast

Read the passage.

Spencer loved writing. He had been practicing with poetry and short stories since he was in first grade. This year, however, he was determined to write an entire chapter book. Spencer started it in September and had written ten chapters already. He showed it to his mom. She finished reading it and said it was fabulous and couldn't wait to see how it ended! ○○○○

Day 1

Clara Brown was born a slave. She got her freedom papers in 1857. However, Clara had only one year to leave the state. If she did not leave, the law said she would become a slave again. At the time, African Americans could not buy tickets for public transportation. **Passage** on a wagon train cost about $500. Clara wanted to go west to search for her daughter Eliza. A wagon master offered her a job as a cook on his wagon train. Clara took the job.

1. What is the meaning of **passage**? _____
_____

2. Why was it important for Clara to leave the state quickly?_____
_____

Day 2

Add the correct punctuation to each sentence.

1. Kate and Luis entered the capsule

2. The Olympic Games were held in Stockholm Sweden in 1912 replied Tisha

3. What is their mission

4. Willie Mae yelled Wow did you see that car

5. Look out screamed Scott

6. Yelena our class president took charge of today's meeting

7. Wynona's dog Bandit is a frisky animal

8. Look out It's an asteroid

Day 3

Circle the correct word.

1. (Too/To/Two) dollars is a (fare/fair) price.

2. Dad (scent/sent) Mom (flours/flowers) for her birthday.

3. We have (too/two) more (weaks/weeks) until this is (dew/due).

4. Can you imagine having (eight/ate) uncles and (ants/aunts)?

5. She and Seth did well in every subject (accept/except) history.

6. Uncle Wallace thanked us (for/four) (hour/our) concern.

7. They are on (there/their) way into deep space.

Day 4

Torika's family quickly began eating. Their chopsticks made clicking noises as they grabbed the food. Ruby was nervous about eating with chopsticks. Torika gave her instructions. Ruby finally managed to pick up a piece of chicken. Suddenly, her fingers slipped, and the chicken flew across the table. It landed in Torika's soup with a splash. Everyone smiled. Torika's grandmother patted Ruby on the arm.

1. Do you think Ruby had used chopsticks before? _____

Underline the evidence in the story.

2. Do you think Ruby will want to continue using chopsticks? Why? _____
_____

1. Add the correct punctuation to each sentence.

   The clerk examined the jacket carefully

   Maricela I yelled Help me cheer for our team

   All of the boys in the class passed the test

2. Use each word in a sentence to show its meaning.

   (sale) _____

   _____

   (pair) _____

   _____

   (pale) _____

   _____

3. Reread the text on Day 4. Why did everyone smile?

   _____

   Why did Torika's grandmother pat Ruby on the arm?

   _____

   _____

   Write a review of your favorite book.

   _____

   _____

   _____

   _____

   _____

   _____

   _____

   _____

Fluency Blast

Read the passage.

Wyatt had been going to bed at 8 pm for as long as he could remember. His older brother, who was a teenager, was allowed to stay up until 11 pm. Wyatt didn't think this was very fair. He tried persuading his parents to change his bedtime. They weren't happy about it. Even though he promised to go straight to bed, they wouldn't agree.

○○○○

Day 1

Clara Brown began cooking each morning at 4 am. Travel began by 7 am. The wagon train stopped for a break at noon and started again at 2 pm. Wagons rolled until 5 pm. Oxen pulled a loaded wagon at about two miles per hour (about 3 kph). They traveled about 15 miles per day (about 24 km). It took Clara's wagon train about eight weeks to get to Colorado. The trip was about 680 miles (about 1,094 km). Clara walked the whole way.

1. Why do you think the author included all these details? _____

_____

2. Describe Clara. _____

_____

Day 2

Circle the choice that shows the correct capitalization.

1. A. Fire marshal Seth Lang

   B. Fire Marshal Seth Lang

   C. fire marshal Seth Lang

2. A. My dog's name is pluto.

   B. My Dog's name is pluto.

   C. My dog's name is Pluto.

3. A. Is Mr. Irwin your Teacher?

   B. Is mr. Irwin your teacher?

   C. Is Mr. Irwin your teacher?

Day 3

Circle the root in each word.

1. audition   2. rejection

3. multiple   4. inspection

5. conform   6. judicial

7. century   8. aquarium

Day 4

Ruby was embarrassed that she couldn't use her chopsticks well. Torika's grandmother gave her a fork and knife. Ruby was relieved. She ate the rest of her dinner easily. It was delicious! After dinner, everyone was given a fortune cookie. Ruby broke hers open, and it read, "If you practice hard, you will learn many things." Ruby laughed and said, "If you let me take home a pair of chopsticks, my fortune may come true!"

1. What did Torika's grandmother do to make Ruby feel comfortable? _____

_____

2. How would you describe Ruby? _____

_____

1. Underline the words that need to be capitalized.

   i received the book the *life cycle of cats* from grandmother.

   will judge myra wolf preside today?

   "dad, the *los angeles times* was not delivered this morning," said dave.

2. Circle the root in each word.

   destruction   video   consent   multimedia

   admit   vocal   bicycle   transportation

3. Reread the text on Day 4. Why did Ruby laugh about her fortune?

   _____

   How do you think this story would be different if Ruby was the narrator?

   _____

   _____

   _____

Write a letter to your parents convincing them to change your bedtime.

_____

_____

_____

_____

_____

_____

_____

_____

Fluency Blast

Read the passage.

Neil and Lee were next-door neighbors and had been attending the same schools all of their lives. Lee had just found out that his parents decided to move across town. Even though they would still be fairly close, both boys knew they probably wouldn't see each other very often. Lee was secretly hoping his parents would change their minds. ○○○○

Day 1

Lewis and Clark's exploration led to fur trading in the West. Several companies competed with each other. They sold **pelts** around the world. They had to hire men to get furs for them. The trappers, who trapped deer, beaver, and muskrat, became known as mountain men. People of different races worked together in the fur trade. One of those men was an African American named James Beckwourth. His mother was a slave.

1. Did the fur trade give everyone an equal opportunity? _____

2. What is a **pelt**? _____

3. Why do you think they were called mountain men? _____

Day 2

Circle the choices that show the correct capitalization.

1. A. Teacher David Taylor

   B. teacher David Taylor

   C. teacher David taylor

2. A. She lives in North Carolina.

   B. She Lives in North Carolina.

   C. She lives in North carolina.

3. A. is Maria going with Mrs. Hammond?

   B. Is maria going with mrs. Hammond?

   C. Is Maria going with Mrs. Hammond?

Day 3

Circle the roots in each word.

1. chronological   2. biology

3. telegram   4. homonym

5. dehydrate   6. psychology

7. perimeter   8. microbe

Day 4

It was almost time for the play to begin, but the lead actress had not arrived. When the door opened, everyone looked up, expecting to see Nora. "I hate to put a damper on things, but Nora has a fever and will not make it tonight," explained her mom. "Well, I never put all of my eggs in one basket," responded Ms. Kaplan. "Sasha has been our understudy for that part and knows it well. Sasha, put on Nora's costume."

1. Where does the story take place?

   _____

2. Who is Ms. Kaplan? _____

   _____

3. How does Ms. Kaplan respond to the problem?

   _____

Name _____

Week 22 Assessment

1. Write two sentences that contain proper nouns.

   _____

   _____

   _____

   _____

2. Circle the root in each word.

   monologue   philosophy   phone   psychic

   thermal   symphony   hypothermia   chronic

3. Reread the text on Day 4. List each idiom and its meaning.

   _____

   _____

   _____

   _____

   _____

   _____

Write a paragraph describing your best friend.

_____

_____

_____

_____

_____

_____

_____

_____

Fluency Blast

Read the passage.

Kaylen loves children, especially small babies. She had been babysitting for her cousins for two years. She asked her parents if she could make flyers to hand out in the neighborhood, and they agreed as long as Kaylen took a babysitting class. She looked online and found one. She could hardly wait to finish so she could babysit for her neighbors!

○○○○

Day 1

James Beckwourth grew up in Missouri. His father taught him to ride horses, work the land, cook, fish, and track game. In 1818, at 20 years old, he began exploring the West. James lived with Native American tribes and learned how to trap beaver and otter. He worked as a scout for a fur company and married a Crow woman named Pine Leaf. He found a pass through the Sierra Nevada Mountains. It was an important route for wagon trains going to California.

1. Describe James Beckwourth.

   _____

2. What important discovery did James make?

   _____

   _____

Day 2

Combine the clauses to create one sentence.

1. Myong wanted to go swimming. It rained.

   _____

   _____

2. Ann brushed her teeth. Ann washed her face.

   _____

   _____

3. The car broke down. I took a taxi.

   _____

   _____

4. The baby cried. The baby was hungry.

   _____

   _____

Day 3

Circle the prefixes in each word.

1. antibiotic

2. devalue

3. discovery

4. indirect

5. important

6. overeat

7. subway

8. unusual

Day 4

Sasha was on cloud nine after the performance. She greeted her family who were waiting at the back of the auditorium. "You were terrific!" said her dad. Sasha was speechless as everyone complimented her. Her dad said, "It's raining cats and dogs outside. Grandpa, keep an eye on everyone while I run and get the car." Finally, her dad returned. "Sorry it took so long. The traffic is slower than molasses."

1. Was Sasha pleased with her performance? How do you know? _____

   _____

2. Underline all of the idioms. Why did the author include them? _____

   _____

1. Rewrite each of the following sentences as two simple sentences.

   The boy started a new painting while his first painting was drying.

   _____

   _____

   While he was waiting for the train, Blaine listened to the street musician.

   _____

   _____

2. Circle the prefixes.

   foreshadow   irrelevant   preview   rewrite

   superhuman   semifinal   underestimate   midfield

3. Reread the text on Day 4. What is the theme of this text?

   _____

   What other books have you read with this theme?

   _____

   _____

   Write a paragraph comparing your favorite fruit to your favorite vegetable.

   _____

   _____

   _____

   _____

   _____

   _____

   _____

   _____

   _____

 CD-104981 • © Carson-Dellosa

Fluency Blast

Read the passage.

One of the most violent storms is a tornado. A tornado is a rotating column of air that extends from a thunderstorm to the ground. Thunderstorms that form in warm, moist air in advance of a cold front might have hail, strong wind, or tornados. Staying aware is important for safety. Look for dark skies, large hail, loud roars, and flash floods.

○○○○

Day 1

In 1838, the United States Government made the Cherokee move from their homes in Georgia and other states to what was then called the **Indian Territory**. That land is now the state of Oklahoma. The Cherokee had to walk for hundreds of miles, and they often did not have enough food or water. Many hundreds of them died. The mothers felt so sad that some of them could not take care of their children.

1. What caused the Cherokee to move?

_____

2. What is the **Indian Territory** called today?

_____

3. This trip is called the Trail of Tears. Underline the clues that tell you why.

Day 2

Combine each pair of simple sentences into a compound sentence.

1. Andrew likes apples. Bobbi likes pears.

_____

_____

2. Bobbi likes skating. Andrew does not like skating.

_____

_____

3. Andrew likes dancing. Bobbi likes singing.

_____

_____

Day 3

Circle the suffixes in each word.

1. affordable   2. tallest

3. helpful   4. sleeping

5. motion   6. activity

7. hopeless   8. lovely

Day 4

My friends and I were having a good time when, out of the blue, Brooke asked me about my trip to Jamaica. A couple of days before, I had lied about going on a trip. Brooke is always bragging about her vacations. For once, I wanted to hold a candle to her, but now I was caught with my foot in my mouth. "What's wrong? Cat got your tongue?" Brooke teased. She knew she had me over a barrel. I asked her to drop it, but she had a one-track mind.

1. What point of view is this? _____

Underline the words in the text that tell you.

2. How would the text be different if Brooke were the narrator? _____

_____

1. Write two compound sentences about your family.

   _____

   _____

   _____

2. Circle the suffix in each word.

   incredible   universal   golden   teacher

   openness   courageous   trenches   gloomy

3. Reread the text on Day 4. Find the idioms. Record each one by its literal meaning.

   A. be compared equally to _____

       _____

   B. without warning _____

       _____

   C. focused only on one thing _____

       _____

   D. saying something you wish you could take back _____

       _____

   ✏️ **Describe a storm that you have seen.**

   _____

   _____

   _____

   _____

   _____

   _____

   _____

   _____

   _____

Fluency Blast

Read the passage.

Ursula was lying in bed when it began to thunder. She had never liked storms because of the loud thunder and bright lightning. She closed her eyes and hoped it wouldn't last very long. After one unusually loud clap of thunder, she bolted out of her bed and sprinted to her parents' room. She watched television with them until the storm was over.

○○○○

Day 1

According to **legend**, the Cherokee chiefs asked the Great One for a sign that would make mothers feel strong enough to care for their children on the Trail of Tears. The Great One promised that when a mother's tear fell, a flower would grow. It is called the Cherokee rose. It is white, which stands for the mothers' tears. The flower's center is gold, a symbol of the gold taken from their land.

1. What does **legend** mean? _____

_____

2. How did the legend of the Cherokee rose come about? _____

_____

_____

Day 2

1. Which of the following contains two **simple** sentences?

   A. He is wearing his baseball uniform. He is holding his baseball bat.

   B. He is wearing his baseball uniform and holding his baseball bat..

2. Which of the following contains a **compound** sentence?

   A. She is eating a salad. She is drinking lemonade.

   B. She is eating a salad, and she is drinking lemonade.

Day 3

Write the meaning of each root.

1. aqua _____

2. aud _____

3. form _____

4. fract _____

5. jud _____

6. multi _____

7. scribe _____

8. spect _____

Day 4

Mariah got a Venus flytrap for her birthday. She put it with her other plants on her windowsill. She watered all of her plants daily. After a week, all of her plants looked fine except for the Venus flytrap. She decided that she needed more information on this plant, so she went to the library and found a book about the Venus flytrap. She took it straight home and read **unremittingly**, skipping dinner and staying up late into the night.

1. What is the meaning of **unremittingly**?

_____

2. How would you describe Mariah?

_____

1. Which of the following is a complex sentence?

   A. Ivy went jogging. Jayla went jogging.

   B. Ivy and Jayla went jogging.

   C. Before breakfast, Ivy and Jayla went jogging.

2. Look at Day 3. Write words using the roots listed. Use each root once.

   _____   _____   _____   _____

   _____   _____   _____   _____

3. Reread the text on Day 1. Think about the Trail of Tears. Describe what you might have seen.

   _____

   _____

   _____

   _____

4. Reread the text on Day 4. Write a title for it.

   _____

Write a story about a new student beginning fifth grade.

   _____

   _____

   _____

   _____

   _____

   _____

   _____

   _____

   _____

⚡ Fluency Blast

Read the passage.

Philip loved taking care of animals. After his teacher got a class hamster, he studied about them and presented a report. The class created a chart, and the students took turns taking care of her. As a group, they suggested names and voted. Athena won by a landslide. Mr. Walker said that was because they had just studied Greek mythology. ○○○○

Day 1

George Washington Carver was born in 1861. His parents were slaves. They lived on a plantation in Missouri. He was often sick as a child. He couldn't help around the plantation. He liked to spend time in the woods. There, he found flowers and plants. He made a collection of them. George taught himself to read. He was very independent. When he was 10 years old, he left the plantation to live on his own.

1. Who do you think George was named after?
   _____

2. How do you know George was independent?
   _____

3. How would you describe George? _____
   _____

Day 2

Rewrite each pair of simple sentences as a compound or complex sentence.

1. George went on a hiking trip. Jay went on a hiking trip.
   _____
   _____

2. We hiked on our long weekend away. We biked on our long weekend away.
   _____
   _____

3. I ate an orange for breakfast. The orange was sweet.
   _____
   _____

Day 3

Write the meaning of each root.

1. auto _____
2. bio _____
3. chron _____
4. gram _____
5. graph _____
6. hydr _____
7. logy _____
8. micro _____

Day 4

Mariah was surprised to find out that her Venus flytrap was carnivorous, or meat eating. No wonder it was not doing well! Each set of leaves stays open until an insect or piece of meat lands on the inside of the leaves. The two leaves close quickly, trapping the **bait** inside. After a leaf digests the meat, it dies. A new leaf grows to take the place of the dead leaf. Now, Mariah knew how to care for her Venus flytrap.

1. What is the meaning of **bait**? _____
   _____

2. Would a Venus flytrap eat a mosquito? Why or why not? _____
   _____
   _____

1. Rewrite the simple sentences as a compound or complex sentence.

   Isabelle walked through the foggy forest.

   Isabelle walked slowly.

   _____

   _____

2. Look at Day 3. Write words using the roots listed. Use each root once.

   _____   _____   _____   _____

   _____   _____   _____   _____

3. Reread the text on Day 4. How does a Venus flytrap catch its food?

   _____

   _____

   What could the author add to help the reader? Why would that help?

   _____

   _____

   _____

Write a letter to your teacher persuading him or her to get a class pet.

_____

_____

_____

_____

_____

_____

_____

Fluency Blast

Read the passage.

Gregory and Colby lived next door to each other and loved spending time together. Mr. Zimmerman, who lived up the street, was teaching the boys how to build things. Their current project was a birdfeeder, and since Colby's mom loved to watch birds, they had agreed to give it to her once it was finished. They couldn't wait to see her reaction! ○○○○

Day 1

George Washington Carver wanted to go to a college. The college refused to admit him because he was African American. But, George refused to give up. Finally, he went to college. He was an excellent student. He took botany and chemistry classes. George became a scientist. He discovered more than 300 uses for the peanut plant. Among his discoveries were shampoo, soap, rubber, wood filler, paint, and shoe polish. His research helped farmers.

1. Underline the words in the text that tell you George was a hard worker.

2. What was the effect of George's research?

   _____

   _____

Day 2

Rewrite each pair of simple sentences as a compound or complex sentence.

1. The class is going on a camping trip. The class will go unless it rains.

   _____

   _____

2. Fred went to the carnival on Saturday. Ethan went to the carnival on Saturday.

   _____

   _____

3. The popcorn crackled as it popped. The popcorn snapped as it popped.

   _____

   _____

Day 3

Write the meaning of each root.

1. mono _____
2. morph _____
3. phobia _____
4. phone _____
5. photo _____
6. psycho _____
7. scope _____
8. therm _____

Day 4

You are my love, my love you are.
I worship you from afar;
I, through the branches, spy you.
I love your ears, so soft and tall.
I love your nose, so pink and small.
I must make you my own bride!

1. What do you think the narrator is talking to?

   _____

   Underline the words in the text that tell you.

2. How does the narrator feel?

   _____

3. What type of text is this?

   _____

1. Rewrite the simple sentences as a compound or complex sentence.

India investigated the old trunk.

The trunk was brown.

_____

_____

2. Look at Day 3. Write words using the roots listed. Use each root once.

_____   _____   _____   _____

_____   _____   _____   _____

3. Reread the text on Day 1. What character traits did George have?

_____

_____

Write a title for the text.

_____

Write a paragraph about something you collect.

_____

_____

_____

_____

_____

_____

_____

CD-104981 • © Carson-Dellosa

Fluency Blast

Read the passage.

Miranda loved learning new things. Her parents had let her take many classes. She could knit a warm scarf, bake a tasty birthday cake, paint creative landscapes, and make beautiful jewelry. She was having a hard time deciding what to tackle next. Maybe she would learn how to play the piano or speak another language.

○○○○

Day 1

In 1868, the Grand Army of the Republic organized a ceremony at the National Cemetery in Arlington, Virginia. They called it Decoration Day because they decorated the graves of soldiers. It was changed to Memorial Day in honor of those who gave their lives for freedom. On November 11, 1918, a treaty was signed putting an end to World War I. It was first called **Armistice** Day, but it is now called Veterans Day.

1. What does **armistice** mean?

    A. beginning of war

    B. parties agree to end war

2. Which two words would you emphasize in the last sentence? _____

Day 2

Rewrite each pair of simple sentences as a compound or complex sentence.

1. Ty excitedly spoke about his journey. Ty loudly spoke about his journey.

    _____

    _____

2. We can stop for breakfast. We can stop if we do it quickly.

    _____

    _____

3. My ice cream melted. My ice cream fell off the cone.

    _____

    _____

Day 3

Write the meaning of each prefix.

1. anti- _____

2. de- _____

3. dis- _____

4. fore- _____

5. mid- _____

6. non- _____

7. pre- _____

8. re- _____

Day 4

You are a climbing ace.
But, I do not like your fuzzy face.
Away from me, please take you!
I will not climb, I cannot eat
the acorns that you call a treat.
Now, **shimmy** up that tree and hide!

1. What do you think the narrator is talking to?

    _____

    Underline the words in the text that tell you.

2. How does the narrator feel?

    _____

3. What is the meaning of **shimmy**?

    _____

1. Rewrite the simple sentences as a compound or complex sentence.

   I saw a spider crawl under the couch.

   The spider was furry.

   _____

   _____

2. Look at Day 3. Write words using the prefixes listed. Use each prefix once.

   _____ _____ _____ _____

   _____ _____ _____ _____

3. Reread the text on Day 1. Why was Memorial Day originally called Decoration Day?

   _____

   _____

   Why do you think they changed the name?

   _____

   _____

If you could learn how to do anything, what would it be and why?

_____

_____

_____

_____

_____

_____

_____

Fluency Blast

Read the passage.

Sasha was up extremely late with her cousins. They hadn't seen each other in over two years. They were excited to be together. Their parents decided to take a vacation to Florida, and the cousins knew they would have a great week! Sasha wanted to collect seashells, build sandcastles, and bodysurf in the ocean.

○ ○ ○ ○

Day 1

A tarantula is a **big**, **hairy** spider. You might see one in a pet shop that carries unusual pets. In the United States, tarantulas live in the West where it is hot and dry. During the day, tarantulas sleep in holes and other dark places. Tarantulas catch their food mostly by jumping on it and biting it. Smaller tarantulas eat insects. Larger ones eat mice and lizards. A tarantula's venom can kill the animals it hunts, but its venom cannot kill a human.

1. Give antonyms for **big** and **hairy**.

   _____

2. If you visit a pet shop that carries unusual pets, you might see

   A. a cat.   B. a canary.   C. a tarantula.

Day 2

Read each sentence. Write **D** if the sentence is declarative, **I** if it is interrogative, **E** if it is exclamatory, and **IM** if it is imperative.

1. _____ Walk up the steps and then turn left.

2. _____ The weather is fantastic!

3. _____ Three bridges cross the Grand Canal.

4. _____ Did your dad make salad for dinner?

5. _____ What a beautiful bridge that is!

6. _____ How warm does it get in the summer?

7. _____ She jogged through the mist.

8. _____ Do you want to go for a walk?

Day 3

Write the meaning of each suffix.

1. –able _____

2. –er _____

3. –est _____

4. –ful _____

5. –tion _____

6. –less _____

7. –ment _____

8. –es _____

Day 4

Brantley and Ava were walking home after school when they found a puppy. She was lying on the sidewalk, and it appeared that her paw was bleeding. When they went to help her, she began to growl. Ava called their mom and she came to help. They took the puppy to the vet, who fixed her paw and gave her shots. Brantley promised to be responsible if Mom would let them keep her. Mom finally gave the **green light** and the arguing about a name began.

1. Why do you think the puppy growled?

   _____

2. What is meant by **green light**?

   _____

   _____

1. Read each sentence. Write **D** if the sentence is declarative, **I** if it is interrogative, **E** if it is exclamatory, and **IM** if it is imperative.

_____ Who is your favorite coach?

_____ Farm Sanctuary rescues animals.

_____ Put your shoes on.

_____ I love to ride roller coasters!

_____ Be careful when you cross the street.

2. Look at Day 3. Write words using the suffixes listed. Use each suffix once.

_____   _____   _____   _____

_____   _____   _____   _____

3. Reread the text on Day 1. What fact might make you feel better about meeting a tarantula?

_____

_____

When a tarantula hunts, what actually kills the animals?

_____

_____

Write a paragraph about what you would do at the beach.

_____

_____

_____

_____

_____

_____

_____

_____

_____

_____

Fluency Blast

Read the passage.

"The Little Mermaid" is a fairy tale written by Hans Christian Andersen. He was born poor in 1805. What extra money the family had, they spent at the theater. When they didn't have money for tickets, Hans would quietly sit outside the theater reading the playbill. He knew he would follow his love of books and the theater as a career. He wrote more than 150 fairy tales.   ○○○○

Day 1

If you are bitten by a tarantula, you soon know that it hurts only about as much as a beesting. Its bite helps the spider protect itself. The **bashful** tarantula bites humans only if it feels threatened and cannot get away. A tarantula has another way to protect itself. It can rub its hind legs together, which causes its stiff leg hairs to fly up in the air. Each tiny hair can cause a hurtful skin or eye wound.

1. What does the author say a tarantula bite feels like? _____

2. Poking or touching a tarantula might make it

   A. run away.   B. bite you.

3. What is another word that means the same as **bashful**? _____

Day 2

Circle the correct adjective.

1. Of the three bats, Joshua's is the (light/lightest).

2. Holly has a very (cute/cuter) kitten.

3. My notebook is (bigger/biggest) than yours.

4. (Light/Lightest) rain fell on the roof.

5. Every mother thinks her child is the (cute/cutest).

6. Jawan's sandwich is (big/bigger) than Evan's.

7. This is the (lighter/lightest) jacket in my closet.

8. His job is (more/most) important than ours.

9. They are (loud/louder) than the morning class.

Day 3

Read each pair of words. Write **S** for synonyms, **A** for antonyms, or **H** for homophones.

1. _____ same, equal

2. _____ pane, pain

3. _____ old, new

4. _____ old, ancient

5. _____ same, different

6. _____ heel, heal

7. _____ grate, great

8. _____ nap, doze

Day 4

Beth did not want to get out of bed. Her big science test was today and she had not studied one bit. She thought if she pretended to be sick her mom might let her stay home in bed. Beth would love that! She could watch television and play video games. When Beth heard her mother outside her door, she began coughing loudly and curled up in a ball. As her mom walked through the door, Beth moaned.

1. How would you describe Beth? Support your answer. _____

   _____

2. Will staying home help Beth? Explain your answer. _____

   _____

1. Write two sentences with comparative or superlative adjectives.

   _____

   _____

   _____

   _____

2. Write a synonym for each word.

   funny   _____   kind   _____

   mean   _____   miserable   _____

3. Reread the text on Day 1. What details does the author use to describe tarantula hairs?

   _____

   _____

   If you saw a tarantula rubbing its legs together, what might happen?

   _____

   _____

Write about your favorite author. What makes him or her your favorite?

   _____

   _____

   _____

   _____

   _____

   _____

   _____

   _____

   _____

Fluency Blast

Read the passage.

The Aboriginal people in Australia are hunters and gatherers. They are also skilled artists. They have been painting and carving rocks for thousands of years. The paintings are found mostly in caves. The oldest paintings that have been discovered are about 30,000 years old. They used paint made from the earth, tree bark, and plants.

○○○○

Day 1

Imagine you're trying to get home. A storm has been **raging** for hours. The sea has been tossing your small sailing craft up and down, and you are not sure where you are. Suddenly, in the distance, you see a faint light. You know you are safe and almost home. Lighthouses were built to guide ships into coastal waters. They were built at dangerous points on coastlines, usually near reefs or at entrances to harbors.

1. Why were lighthouses useful? _____

_____

_____

2. What is the meaning of **raging**?

_____

Day 2

Read each sentence. Write **C** if it is a comparative adjective and **S** if it is a superlative adjective.

1. _____ The most challenging competition is the World Cup.

2. _____ The World Cup can be played in some of the worst weather.

3. _____ Athletes have more specialized training now.

4. _____ They are the best team in South America.

5. _____ England has a better team this year.

6. _____ The more training a team has, the better they will be.

Day 3

Read each pair of words. Write **S** for synonyms, **A** for antonyms, or **H** for homophones.

1. _____ to, too

2. _____ near, close

3. _____ angry, mad

4. _____ energetic, lazy

5. _____ dawn, dusk

6. _____ stroll, walk

7. _____ keep, give

8. _____ whisper, holler

Day 4

A jay wandered into a yard where peacocks walked and found a number of feathers on the ground. He tied them all to his tail and strutted toward the peacocks. When he neared them, the peacocks discovered what he'd done. They strode to him and pecked at him, plucking away his borrowed feathers. The jay returned to the other jays. They were equally annoyed at him and said, "It is not only fine feathers that make fine birds."

1. Why did the jay tie the feathers to his tail?

_____

2. Why were the peacocks upset with the jay?

_____

_____

1. Write two sentences about sports using comparative or superlative adjectives.

_____

_____

_____

_____

2. Write an antonym for each word.

funny _____   kind _____

dark _____   miserable _____

3. Reread the text on Day 4. What is the theme?

_____

_____

What other stories have you read with the same theme?

_____

_____

Write about your favorite sport.

_____

_____

_____

_____

_____

_____

_____

_____

 CD-104981 • © Carson-Dellosa

Fluency Blast

Read the passage.

Most people welcome a new invention that makes life easier. When the cotton gin arrived in 1793, it was the slaves' worst nightmare. At that time, people weren't making as much money as they wanted from their crops. One kind of cotton was hard to de-seed, but it would grow anywhere. Eli Whitney invented the cotton gin to help with this.

○○○○

Day 1

Boston Light was built in 1716. It was the first lighthouse in the colonies. By the time the Declaration of Independence was signed in 1776, the United States had 12 lighthouses, mainly in New England. In 1800, the United States had 16 lighthouses, and by 1812, it had about 49 lighthouses. The first West Coast lighthouses were completed in 1854 and 1855 in California.

1. What would be a good title for this text?

_____

2. Why do you think so many lighthouses were built during the colonial days?

_____

_____

Day 2

Complete each sentence with the following correlative or coordinating conjunctions: **and, but, or, both, either, neither, nor**.

1. Avery wanted to have pretzels as a snack _____ Amira wanted snowcones.

2. _____ Colby _____ Eli wanted to tell Sandy the bad news.

3. We were going to see a movie, _____ we went out to eat instead.

4. Do you want apple pie _____ blueberry pie?

5. We can _____ run _____ ride our bikes to get there on time.

Day 3

Read each pair of words. Write **S** for synonyms, **A** for antonyms, or **H** for homophones.

1. _____ large, small

2. _____ large, huge

3. _____ tiny, miniscule

4. _____ through, threw

5. _____ see, sea

6. _____ rode, road

7. _____ flee, flea

8. _____ fall, stand

Day 4

A hungry wolf spied a goat browsing at the top of a steep cliff. "That is a very dangerous place for you," he called out, pretending to be very anxious about the goat's safety. "What if you should fall? Please come down and get the finest grass in the country." The goat looked over the edge of the cliff. "How very, very **anxious** you are about me," she said, "and how generous you are with your grass! But, I know it's your own appetite you are thinking of!"

1. What is the meaning of **anxious**?

_____

2. Why does the wolf want the goat to come down from the cliff? _____

_____

1. Write two sentences with coordinating conjunctions. Circle the conjunctions.

   _____

   _____

   _____

   _____

2. Use each homophone in a sentence to show its meaning.

   through _____

   _____

   threw _____

   _____

3. Reread the text on Day 1. Create a timeline with information from the text.

   ├───┤

   Write about a time you have felt anxious.

   _____

   _____

   _____

   _____

   _____

   _____

   _____

   _____

   _____

   _____

Fluency Blast

Read the passage.

Eli Whitney sized up the cotton situation. Within a short time, this brilliant young man invented the cotton gin. The gin detached the seeds from the soft, cottony fibers. The sturdy, inland cotton could quickly be de-seeded. The machine was unbelievably simple. It used wires, a drum, and a brush. Growing cotton could now make a lot of money. ○○○○

Day 1

One of the main parts of your brain is the cerebrum. Perhaps you have heard someone talk about **gray matter** while discussing intelligence. This refers to the cerebrum. It is large, and its outside layer, called the cerebral cortex, is gray and looks wrinkled. The cerebrum and the cerebral cortex spring to work when you are doing something that requires a good deal of thought. If you are taking a test or talking to a friend, your cerebrum is busy.

1. What is the main idea of this text? _____

   _____

2. Why is the cerebrum referred to as **gray matter**? _____

   _____

Day 2

Complete each sentence with one of the following subordinating conjunctions: **as long as, since, because, while, after, until.**

1. Delaina practiced jumping _____ she could before her legs got too tired.

2. Ivan wanted to stay inside and play board games _____ it was still raining.

3. We will eat dessert _____ the main course.

4. The dog waited by the door _____ her owner returned home.

5. Gavin sets the table _____ Javon finishes cooking.

Day 3

Write one synonym and one antonym for each word.

1. small _____ _____

2. happy _____ _____

3. fast _____ _____

4. wet _____ _____

5. nice _____ _____

Day 4

A wolf left his lair one evening in fine spirits and an excellent appetite. As he ran, the setting sun cast his shadow far out on the ground, and it looked as if the wolf were a hundred times bigger than he really was. "Why," exclaimed the wolf proudly, "see how big I am! Fancy me running away from a puny lion! I'll show him who is fit to be king, he or I." Just then an **immense** shadow blocked him out, and the next instant a lion struck him down with a single blow.

1. What is the meaning of the word **immense**?

   _____

2. What made the wolf brave? _____

   _____

   _____

1. Read each sentence. Circle the conjunction. Write **CD** for coordinating or **S** for subordinating.

_____ Neither pasta nor pizza was offered on the menu.

_____ While we are waiting in line, let's get some popcorn.

_____ Are we going to go biking or hiking on Saturday?

2. Reread the text on Day 4. Find a synonym for each word.

large _____   said _____

little _____   saw _____

3. Reread the text on Day 1. How does the author support the fact that the cerebrum supports deep thinking?

_____

_____

What is one thing you did today that required the cerebral cortex?

_____

_____

Write a letter to your teacher trying to get him or her to change something in class. Give reasons to support your opinion.

_____

_____

_____

_____

_____

_____

_____

_____

_____

Fluency Blast

Read the passage.

Plantation owners stopped grumbling about cotton growing because the cotton gin helped them. They began exporting cotton and importing slaves. Who else could work the fields? Who could pick the large amounts of cotton for the super machine? All Eli Whitney wanted was to make life easier. Instead, life for thousands became much harder.

○○○○

Day 1

Each year, citizens of the United States celebrate two holidays to remember men and women who fought in wars. Memorial Day is **celebrated** on the last Monday in May, and Veterans Day is celebrated on November 11. Memorial Day began after the American Civil War, when people began decorating the graves of those who had died in the war. Waterloo, New York, **birthplace** of Memorial Day, held a celebration on May 5, 1866.

1. Circle the synonym for **celebrated** as it is used here.
   A. partied   B. observed
2. What is the topic of this text? _____
   _____

Day 2

Underline the preposition and circle the object in each sentence.

1. Many planets revolve around the sun.
2. Our planet has one moon in orbit.
3. The moon orbits near Earth.
4. The Phoenix landed on Mars.
5. Sometimes, you can see Venus at night.
6. Jupiter is the largest planet in the solar system.
7. You might need to look through a telescope.
8. There are many stars in the night sky.
9. The moon sometimes hides behind some clouds.
10. There is a ring around Saturn.

Day 3

Use each homophone in a sentence that shows its meaning.

1. mist _____
   _____
2. missed _____
   _____
3. seen _____
   _____
4. scene _____
   _____

Day 4

A fox and a leopard amused themselves by **disputing** each other's good looks. The leopard was proud of his glossy, spotted coat. The fox prided himself on his fine, bushy tail, but he was wise enough to see that he could not rival the leopard. Still he argued, just to have fun. The leopard was about to lose his temper when the fox said, "You may be beautiful but you would be a great deal better off if you had a little more smartness. That's what I call real beauty."

1. What is the meaning of **disputing**?
   _____
2. What was the leopard proud of?
   _____
   _____

1. Write two sentences about your desk using prepositions.

   _____

   _____

   _____

   _____

2. What is a homograph?

   _____

   What is a homophone?

   _____

3. Reread the text on Day 1. How did people celebrate the first Memorial Day?

   _____

   _____

   What is the meaning of **birthplace**?

   _____

   _____

Write a review for your favorite movie.

_____

_____

_____

_____

_____

_____

_____

_____

_____

Fluency Blast

Read the passage.

The Statue of Liberty stands on Liberty Island. This is in New York Harbor. She was built in France in 1875. She was presented to the United States on July 4, 1884. Her official name is "Liberty Enlightening the World." Many people come from all over the world to see her. She is a symbol of freedom. She proudly greets visitors coming to America.

○○○○

Day 1

Many cultures have stories telling how the world was created. The Aborigines believe that spirits created the world in a time known as **Dreamtime**. The Aborigines have lived in Australia for thousands of years. Some scientists believe they have been in Australia for about 30,000 years. The name Aborigine means "the very first." The Aborigines were the very first people in Australia. Today, the elders **pass on the Dreamtime stories** to younger generations.

1. What is **Dreamtime**? _____

_____

2. Is Dreamtime still a part of Aboriginal culture today? Explain. _____

_____

Day 2

Underline each prepositional phrase and circle each preposition.

1. The ship sank beneath the frothing waves.
2. The dancers whirled around the crowded, noisy room.
3. The students walked across the street.
4. The dog ran through the yard.
5. The horse jumped over the high fence.
6. The students played outside at the late recess.
7. Do you want to hike up that steep hill?
8. The paper fell underneath the small bookcase.
9. Heath walked out of the scary movie.
10. Ginny looked down the deep well.

Day 3

Use each homograph in a sentence that shows its meaning.

1. bat _____

_____

2. bow _____

_____

3. fine _____

_____

4. lead _____

_____

Day 4

A lion had been watching three bulls eating in an open field. He had tried to attack them several times, but they had kept together and helped each other to drive him off. But, he could not keep away from that field, for it is hard to resist watching a good meal, even when there is little chance of getting it. Then one day, the bulls had a quarrel and were in separate corners of the field. It was now an easy matter for the lion to attack them one at a time.

1. Why did the lion keep going back to the field?

_____

2. What is the theme of this story?

_____

_____

1. Underline each prepositional phrase and circle each preposition.

   The salad greens were piled high in the chilled bowl.

   It's cold, so I'm going to put two blankets on my bed.

2. Use the homograph in sentences that show both meanings.
   tear

   _____

   _____

   _____

   _____

3. Reread the text on Day 1. What does the phrase **pass on the Dreamtime stories** mean?

   _____

   _____

   What other stories have you read that explain how the world was created?

   _____

Write a short fable. Be sure it has a moral.

_____

_____

_____

_____

_____

_____

_____

_____

_____

Fluency Blast

Read the passage.

There are many different birthday traditions. In Rome, they used to celebrate the birthdays of gods. In Britain, they celebrate the Queen's birthday. In the United States, they celebrate the birthdays of important leaders. Most Eastern cultures don't even recognize the date of birth. When the first moon of the new year arrives, everyone is one year older.

○○○○

Day 1

Aborigines believe that spirits created the land, plants, and people. The spirits then continued to live in nature. Dreamtime stories tell more than the **origin** of the world. They explain rules for living, behavior, and society. Dreamtime paintings show these stories. They are usually symmetrical and are made of arcs, circles, and ovals. The men paint Dreamtime symbols and patterns on their bodies for special ceremonies.

1. What is the meaning of **origin**?

_____

2. Why would the men paint these symbols and patterns on their bodies? _____

_____

Day 2

Place each adjective phrase in the correct order.

1. purse red a small

_____

2. large the purple slide

_____

3. brown pretty puppy small

_____

4. apple delicious red

_____

5. blue plate round old

_____

Day 3

Write one simile and one metaphor for each noun.

1. ball

_____

_____

2. sun

_____

_____

3. flower

_____

_____

Day 4

A fox fell into a well, and though it was not very deep, he could not get out. After he had been there a long time, a thirsty goat came by and asked if the water was good. "The finest in the whole country," said the **crafty** fox. "Jump in and try it." The goat immediately jumped in and began to drink. The fox jumped on the goat's back and leaped out of the well. The foolish goat begged the fox to help him out. But, the fox was already on his way to the woods.

1. What is the meaning of **crafty**? _____

_____

2. Describe the goat. _____

_____

Name _____

1. Complete each sentence by inserting adjectives.

   I bought a _____ _____ shirt at the store.

   He gave his mother a _____ _____ flower for Mother's Day.

2. Write **S** for simile or **M** for metaphor.

   _____ The sun was a diamond reflecting off the lake.

   _____ The sun felt as hot as an oven.

3. Reread the text on Day 1.

   Write three facts about Dreamtime.

   _____

   _____

   _____

   Write a title for the text.

   _____

Write about your favorite birthday.

_____

_____

_____

_____

_____

_____

_____

Name _____

Name _____

 Fluency Blast

Read the passage.

   Sue is a Tyrannosaurus rex and she is the largest and best preserved T. rex ever discovered. She resides in Chicago at The Field Museum and is on display for the public to see. Visitors can view her up close. She is quite special because she is the most complete T. rex fossil ever found. We have a lot to learn about our past from Sue because she has given us much to explore. ○○○○

Day 1

   Many African women were **skilled seamstresses**. Many of them knew how to sew before they were brought to America as slaves. Skilled seamstresses sold for a high price on the slavery block. Sometimes, they sold for as much as $1,000. Some slaves made quilts for their owners. They used the scraps from those quilts to make quilts to keep their own families warm. Those quilts often told the stories of their families. The quilts were called **story quilts**.

1. What is a **skilled seamstress**? _____

   _____

2. Why was a skilled seamstress so valuable?

   _____

   _____

Day 2

Use two adjectives to describe each noun.

1. _____ _____ car
2. _____ _____ house
3. _____ _____ school
4. _____ _____ baby
5. _____ _____ ball
6. _____ _____ game
7. _____ _____ boy
8. _____ _____ dress
9. _____ _____ tree
10. _____ _____ bike

Day 3

Write one simile and one metaphor for each noun.

1. dog

   _____

   _____

2. song

   _____

   _____

3. friend

   _____

   _____

Day 4

   Samantha had been playing soccer since she was six years old. Her dad was her first coach. There was a travel team that Samantha wanted to be on, but she had heard it was almost impossible to make it. She practiced every day for two straight months. Her dad took her to the tryouts and cheered for her on the sidelines. Samantha **had given it her all**, but she was afraid she would not make the team.

1. What character traits does Samantha show?

   _____

   _____

2. What is meant by **had given it her all**?

   _____

   _____

1. Write two sentences that each contain at least two adjectives.

   _____

   _____

   _____

   _____

2. Write **S** for simile or **M** for metaphor.

   _____ He ran like the wind because he was late.

   _____ The snow is a blanket covering the ground.

3. Reread the text on Day 1. What is a **story quilt**?

   _____

   _____

   What would be on your family's story quilt? Why?

   _____

   _____

   _____

   _____

Write an acrostic poem about dinosaurs.

_____

_____

_____

_____

_____

_____

_____

_____

_____

Fluency Blast

Read the passage.

Wendy was doing a report on the Milky Way Galaxy. She enjoyed reading about space. She asked the director of the observatory some questions. She wanted to know how many planets orbit the sun. The director told her that there are eight planets that orbit our sun. She also found out that planets are divided into two categories: Earth-like and gaseous.

○○○○

Day 1

The **Underground Railroad** wasn't a railroad at all. It was a group of people who helped slaves escape to freedom. Those in charge of the escape effort were often called conductors. The people escaping were known as passengers. The places where the escaping slaves stopped for help were called **stations**. Those who escaped followed routes that had been laid out before them. Some went underground through dirt tunnels.

1. What was the **Underground Railroad**?

   _____

   _____

2. What are **stations**? _____

   _____

Day 2

Expand each fragment into a complete sentence.

1. takes a walk every day

   _____

   _____

2. because the line was so long

   _____

   _____

3. every day at lunch

   _____

   _____

Day 3

Match each proverb to its meaning.

1. _____ Actions speak louder than words.

2. _____ Too many cooks spoil the soup.

3. _____ Better late than never.

4. _____ Don't judge a book by its cover.

_____

A. It's better to be late than to not do something at all.

B. What you do is more important than what you say.

C. When too many people are involved in a task, it may not be done well.

D. Don't form an opinion based on appearance.

Day 4

A crab once left the seashore and went and settled in a meadow some way inland. It looked very nice and green and seemed likely to be a good place to feed in. But, a hungry fox came along and spied the crab and caught him. Just as he was going to be eaten up, the crab said, "This is just what I deserve; for I had no business to leave my **natural home** by the sea and settle here as though I belonged to the land."

1. Why did the crab leave the seashore?

   _____

   _____

2. What is meant by **natural home**?

   _____

1. Expand each fragment into a complete sentence.

the birthday party

_____

_____

a purple knit sweater

_____

_____

2. Write the meaning of the proverb.

Don't put off until tomorrow what you can do today.

_____

_____

3. Reread the text on Day 4. What is the theme of this text?

_____

What other stories have you read with the same theme?

_____

_____

_____

What did you like most about this school year? Why?

_____

_____

_____

_____

_____

_____

_____

_____

Fluency Blast

Read the passage.

Kevin and Kellie were twins and wanted a brand-new puppy for their birthday. Their mother told them that pets are a huge responsibility, and she didn't think they were ready for it. The twins worked hard around the house for months convincing their mom they could do it. On the morning of their birthday, their parents surprised them with a dalmatian. They were so excited! ○○○○

Day 1

Escaping slaves needed food and water to make the journey. Conductors helped guide them and provide supplies. One of the most famous Underground Railroad conductors was Harriet Tubman. She had escaped slavery herself. Experts disagree about how well the Underground Railroad was organized. Still, it is believed that the system helped thousands of slaves reach freedom between 1830 and 1865.

1. Why do you think Harriet Tubman was a part of the Underground Railroad? _____

_____

2. How did conductors play an important role?

_____

Day 2

Add punctuation where needed.

1. When will you get home

2. Callista said Mr Taylor said to do Lesson Eight for homework

3. Careful the path is very muddy

4. At the M L K School everybody reads Isabelle Allende in sixth grade

5. I want to read my book all day tomorrow

Day 3

Match each proverb to its meaning.

1. _____ Good things come to those who wait.
2. _____ Honesty is the best policy.
3. _____ Knowledge is power.
4. _____ People in glass houses shouldn't throw stones.
5. _____ A picture is worth a thousand words.

_____

A. Don't criticize someone if you're not perfect.
B. If you're patient, good things happen.
C. An image can tell a story better than words.
D. It's always best to tell the truth.
E. The more you know the more power you'll have in life.

Day 4

Joey loved many things. Playing sports, reading, singing, and doing puzzles were her favorites. Her best friend, Cara, shared all of the same interests, and they spent many hours together. Cara's mom got transferred for work, and they had to move far away. Although Joey knew they could talk and email, she was **devastated**. Soon, Joey's mom found a way for them to work on the same puzzle over the internet. Joey couldn't wait to tell Cara!

1. What is the meaning of **devastated**?

_____

2. What is the point of view of this text?

   A. first person   B. second person

         C. third person

1. Rewrite the sentence. Add punctuation where needed.

   Mom yelled Be nice to your sister

   _____

2. Write the meaning of the proverb.

   The grass is always greener on the other side of the fence.

   _____

   _____

3. Reread the text on Day 1. Compare and contrast the Underground Railroad with a normal railroad.

Underground Railroad   normal railroad

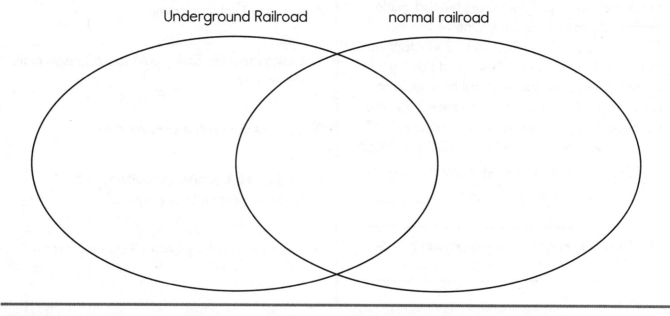

 Write a paragraph about what you think sixth grade will be like.

_____

_____

_____

_____

_____

_____

_____

_____

_____

_____

Fluency Blast

Read the passage.

December is the 12th month of the year. Until 46 BC, it had only 29 days. December has two birthstones. Many holidays are celebrated in December. It is a time many kids have a break from school. People travel to see relatives. The first heavier-than-air flight was on December 17, 1903, in Kitty Hawk, North Carolina.

○○○○

Day 1

Throughout history, people have been faced with **critical choices**. Sometimes, people's choices have made the world a better place for everyone. Sometimes, they have made the world a better place only for themselves. Harriet Tubman's friend, Thomas Garrett, a white businessman, was fined $5,400 (a huge amount in the 1800s) and arrested for his part in the Underground Railroad. Knowing he was doing the right thing, Thomas continued helping.

1. What is the meaning of **critical choices**?

   _____

   _____

2. What is the main idea of this text? _____

   _____

Day 2

Add punctuation where needed.

1. Oh no There has been an accident

2. Can Lynn come over after school I asked

3. Tony and Wren wanted to go to the movies

4. I don't know how to do this Zack complained

5. Hey be careful Quinn yelled

Day 3

Match each idiom to its meaning.

1. _____ sick as a dog
2. _____ jump the gun
3. _____ out of the blue
4. _____ once in a blue moon
5. _____ rub the wrong way

A. doesn't happen often

B. to do something early

C. very ill

D. to annoy someone

E. something that is unexpected

Day 4

A peacock met a crane one day, and to **impress** him, spread his gorgeous tail in the sun. "Look," he said. "What have you to compare with this? I am dressed in all the glory of the rainbow, while your feathers are gray as dust!" The crane spread his broad wings and flew up toward the sun. "Follow me if you can," he said. But, the peacock stood where he was among the birds of the barnyard, while the crane soared in freedom far up into the blue sky.

1. What is the meaning of **impress**? _____

   _____

2. What lesson did the peacock learn?

   _____

   _____

1. Rewrite the sentence. Add punctuation where needed.

   Jeremy wanted to go to the store but Irene wanted to go to the restaurant

   _____

2. Write the meaning of each idiom.

   I'm all ears.

   _____

   hit the hay

   _____

3. Reread the text on Day 1. The author might say that Thomas Garrett made the right critical choice. How is this supported in the text?

   _____

   _____

   _____

   _____

   _____

Write a poem about your teacher.

_____

_____

_____

_____

_____

_____

_____

_____

_____

Answer Key

Page 9
Day 1: 1. similarities and differences between Australia and the United States; 2. winter; 3. left; **Day 2:** 1. Dad; I; park; 2. It's; Car; day; 3. graders'; 4. wait; who's; 5. The; Benjamin's group; **Day 3:** 1–10. Answers will vary. **Day 4:** 1. A; 2. removed; 3. underlined: girl; girls' gym

Page 10
1. there; cars'; That's; too; Which; your; 2. Check students' work. 3. compare/contrast; Answers will vary but should include reference to the paragraph comparing and contrasting Australia and the United States.

Page 11
Day 1: 1. United States; 2. by stating the population numbers of each country; 3. a zoo; **Day 2:** 1. Xun's kindergarten; race, too; 2. your; there; 3. It; they're; cars'; 4. because; apart; 5. Did; Mr. Dolby's; **Day 3:** 1–10. Check students' work. **Day 4:** 1. forget where you put something; 2. suggestions; 3. because she had helped with the report

Page 12
1. It's; I'm; year's; pleased; surprised; piece; 2. Check students' work. 3. Answers will vary but may include that Laura is careless because she misplaced her report. Laura's mom may be described as disappointed because she had helped Laura.

Page 13
Day 1: 1. the government of Australia and the United States; 2. the person in charge of the country; **Day 2:** Check students' work. **Day 3:** 1. A; 2. S; 3. S; 4. A; 5. A; **Day 4:** 1. Answers will vary but may include that she will not remember because she was preoccupied with finding her report. 2. looking through your memory to try to remember

Page 14
1. Check students' work. 2. S; A; S; 3. Answers will vary but may include that one similiarity is that people are elected to the legislature in both countries and one difference is that eligible voters must vote in Australia and in the US it is optional.

Page 15
Day 1: 1. Both are mammals. 2. Marsupials carry babies in pouches. Monotremes give birth by laying eggs. **Day 2:** 1. B; 2. B 3. B; 4. A; 5. A; **Day 3:** 1. allowed; 2. aloud; 3. threw; 4. through; 5. two; to; too; **Day 4:** 1. very good; excellent; 2. He began studying with his sisters every night. 3. Answers will vary but may include they were supportive.

Page 16
1. Did; Around; World; Days; Academy Award; Does; Grandpa; Chicago Sun-Times; Chicago Tribune; We're; Italian; Friday; Strega Nona; 2. A; B; 3. a marsupial; dangerous; They have sharp teeth and eat other mammals, birds, and reptiles.

Page 17
Day 1: 1. It eats crawfish and small fish. 2. soft fur, a snout, webbed feet and claws, and a flat tail; **Day 2:** 1. friends; 2. foxes; 3. cliffs; 4. leaves; 5. cherries; 6. plays; **Day 3:** 1. bear; 2. bare; 3. ate; 4. eight; 5. knew; new; **Day 4:** 1. She is going to volunteer at the animal shelter. 2. A

Page 18
1. cities; keys; birds; 2. B, A; 3. B; Answers will vary.

Answer Key

Page 19

Day 1: 1. Answers will vary. 2. underlined: It is located in Sydney Harbor. 3. a feature of a town or city that is easily recognized; **Day 2:** 1. bosses; 2. countries; 3. boys; 4. roofs; 5. calves; 6. taxes; 7. flies; 8. donkeys; 9. chiefs; 10. wives; **Day 3:** 1. B; 2. B; **Day 4:** 1. poem; 2. Answers will vary but should reference the characteristics of poetry. 3. live

Page 20

1. carrots; waltzes; spiders; knives; churches; cups; wishes; worries; pages; 2. Check students' work. 3. four; It is a three-toed sloth and it has 12 toes. Answers will vary.

Page 21

Day 1: 1. 14 years; 2. $102 million; 3. made of 10 arched-concrete shells; **Day 2:** 1. children; 2. teeth; 3. cacti; 4. feet; 5. oxen; 6. fish or fishes; 7. mice; 8. women; 9. deer; 10. potatoes; **Day 3:** 1. A; 2. B; **Day 4:** 1. swinging slowly back and forth; 2. a dog; 3. autumn; underlined: references to the brown and red leaves and the cool, crisp air

Page 22

1. geese; loaves; men; volcanoes; sheep; people; moose; puppies; dogs; 2. Check students' work. 3. Yes; It is made of shell shapes. to tell us about the Sydney Opera House

Page 23

Day 1: 1. factories; 2. sugar and starch; 3. cells; **Day 2:** Answers will vary. **Day 3:** 1. A; 2. B; **Day 4:** 1. Answers will vary but should include the sounds referenced in the text. 2. older dog; underlined: Shane's graying ears

Page 24

1–2. Check students' work. 3. happy; Check students' work.

Page 25

Day 1: 1. keep; 2. roots; 3. plants; **Day 2:** 1. A; 2. A; 3. C; 4. A; 5. C; 6. C; 7. A; 8. A; 9. C; 10. C; 11. A; 12. A; **Day 3:** 1. S; Garrett – bear in winter; 2. M; grass–cool carpet; 3. M; Aunt Heather– mama bear; **Day 4:** 1. going down in number; 2. He is excited to learn about them. underlined: references to facts about the wombats

Page 26

1. something that can be experienced with your five senses; an idea or concept; 2. Check students' work. 3. descriptive; Answers will vary but may include how they use carbon dioxide to release oxygen back into the air.

Page 27

Day 1: 1. a window; 2. to tell how a TV works; 3. Answers will vary. **Day 2:** 1. are; 2. is; 3. correct; 4. are; 5. correct; **Day 3:** 1. M; moon – plump, friendly face; 2. M; highway – parking lot; 3. S; brother – molasses; **Day 4:** 1. to get her to sing and drop the treat; 2. No, he just wanted the treat.

Page 28

1. needs; give; is; 2. Check students' work. 3. Answers will vary but may include you should not always trust someone who gives you a compliment. A picture could be added showing the crow losing her treat.

Page 29

Day 1: 1. getting things ready for something to happen; 2. V. Zworykin; 3. 1929; **Day 2:** 1–5. Check students' work. **Day 3:** 1. M; Kenyon – night owl; 2. S; wildflowers – confetti; 3. M; moon – shadow; **Day 4:** 1. as scared as a turkey on Thanksgiving; scared; 2. fiction; a fictional letter; 3. her little sister

CD-104981 • © Carson-Dellosa

Answer Key

Page 30

1–2. Check students' work. 3. chronologically; 100 years; Answers will vary but may include probably not since the idea was so new and not everyone could afford the new technology.

Page 31

Day 1: 1. the modern television; 2. Answers will vary but may include curious and smart. 3. Check students' work. **Day 2:** 1. are walking; 2. was going; 3. will be watching; 4. was sleeping; 5. am taking; **Day 3:** 1–3. Check students' work. **Day 4:** 1. table of contents; 2. chronologically; 3. autumn, Answers will vary but may include that school begins in autumn and farmers harvest crops in autumn.

Page 32

1–2. Check students' work. 3. Answers will vary but should reference snow. Check students' work.

Page 33

Day 1: 1. Philo Farnsworth and how television works; 2. Answers will vary but should reference his patents. **Day 2:** 1. P; 2. PR; 3. F; 4. PR; 5. P; **Day 3:** 1–2. Check students' work.
Day 4: 1. Answers will vary but should include the oak thinking he is better than the reeds.
2. stood tall in a proud way

Page 34

1–4. Check students' work.

Page 35

Day 1: 1. It is important. 2. by listing its functions; **Day 2:** 1. should; 2. must; 3. Will; 4. should; 5. might; **Day 3:** 1. very kind; 2. something we wait for seems to take forever; 3. a picture shows something better than a bunch of words; 4. a very small amount; 5. to forget;
Day 4: 1. strong winds; 2. pride; The oak was not able to withstand the hurricane.

Page 36

1–2. Check students' work. 3. Answers will vary but should reference pride. Answers will vary but should reference the differences between fiction and nonfiction.

Page 37

Day 1: 1. hardened dead cells; 2. root; follicle; hair shaft; **Day 2:** 1. FP; 2. PP; 3. PP; 4. PR; 5. FP;
Day 3: 1. don't put all your resources into one thing; 2. it cost a lot; 3. money you don't spend is money saved; 4. behave better; 5. change your mind; **Day 4:** 1. easy; 2. not very good;
3. underlined: Raul was more of an albatross than an eagle.

Page 38

1–3. Check students' work.

Page 39

Day 1: 1. the structure of hair; 2. Yes, with hair straighteners and perms; 3. Answers will vary.
Day 2: 1. have watched; 2. had noticed; 3. had gone; 4. have been excited; 5. have been adding; **Day 3:** 1. C; 2. A; 3. E; 4. B; 5. D; **Day 4:** 1–2. Check students' work.

Page 40

1. will have built; will have stocked; have added;
2. Check students' work. 3. Answers will vary but may include you can't always teach something to someone.

Page 41

Day 1: 1. chronologically; 2. Answers will vary but may include hard. **Day 2:** 1–4. Check students' work. **Day 3:** 1. C; 2. E; 3. B; 4. A; 5. D; **Day 4:** 1. a cat; 2. Answers will vary but may include she has a quiet purr. 3. simile: tongue is like fine grains of sand; metaphors: She is an electric sander. She is a nail file.

Answer Key

Page 42
1–2. Check students' work. 3. poem; Answers will vary but may include that she is licking her owner.

Page 43
Day 1: 1. how free African Americans were treated; 2. made, set; 3. 400,000;
Day 2: 1. unloaded; 2. stay; 3. is; 4. started; 5. warmed; **Day 3:** 1. I; 2. S; 3. P; 4. P; 5. M; 6. I; 7. M; 8. S; **Day 4:** 1. the usual way; 2. Answers will vary but may include soup and rice.

Page 44
1. burned; will meet; 2. Check students' work. 3. Answers will vary but may include so they would not be able to advance in the workplace.

Page 45
Day 1: 1. She wanted to go to Colorado to find her daughter. 2. papers to prove she wasn't a runaway slave; **Day 2:** planned; applied; was; threw; will miss; look; **Day 3:** our; 2. lies; 3. Effects; except; 4. laid; 5. laid; 6. due; week; 7. eight flowers; **Day 4:** 1. Check students' work. 2. good for you; healthy

Page 46
1. C; N; N; 2. Check students' work. 3. rice; Answers will vary but should reference using silverware.

Page 47
Day 1: 1. travel fare; 2. She only had one year to leave the state or she would be a slave again.
Day 2: 1. Kate and Luis entered the capsule. 2. "The Olympic Games were held in Stockholm, Sweden in 1912," replied Tisha. 3. What is their mission? 4. Willie Mae yelled, "Wow! Did you see that car?" 5. "Look out!" screamed Scott. 6. Yelena, our class president, took charge of today's meeting. 7. Wynona's dog, Bandit, is a frisky animal. 8. Look out! It's an asteroid!
Day 3: 1. Two; fair; 2. sent; flowers; 3. two; weeks; due; 4. eight; aunts; 5. except; 6. for; our; 7. their; **Day 4:** No. She was nervous about using chopsticks. 2. Answers will vary but may

include that she will want to with the family supporting her.

Page 48
1. The clerk examined the jacket carefully. "Maricela," I yelled. "Help me cheer for our team." All of the boys in the class passed the test. 2. Check students' work. 3. Answers will vary but may include that they thought it was cute. Torika's grandmother may have patted Ruby's arm to reassure her.

Page 49
Day 1: 1. Answers will vary but should include how hard the trip was. 2. Answers will vary but should include Clara being a hard worker. **Day 2:** 1. B; 2. C; 3. C; **Day 3:** 1. aud; 2. ject; 3. multi; 4. spect; 5. form; 6. jud; 7. cent; 8. aqua; **Day 4:** 1. She gave her a fork and a knife. 2. Answers will vary but may include that she still didn't give up on using chopsticks.

Page 50
1. I; The Life Cycle; Cats; Grandmother; Will Judge Myra Wolf; Dad; Los Angeles Times; Dave; 2. struct; vid; sent; multi; mit; voc; cycl; port; 3. Answers will vary but may include that Ruby did need to practice hard to use chopsticks. If Ruby were the narrator she may have expressed more inner thoughts about the dinner.

Page 51
Day 1: 1. Yes; 2. fur; 3. Answers will vary but may include that deer, beaver, and muskrats can be found in the mountains. **Day 2:** 1. B; 2. A; 3. C; **Day 3:** 1. chron; 2. bio; logy; 3. tele; gram; 4. homo; 5. hydra; 6. psych; logy; 7. meter; 8. micro; **Day 4:** 1. backstage at a theater; 2. the director; 3. She tells Sasha to put on Nora's costume.

Page 52
1. Check students' work. 2. mono; phil; phon; psych; therm; phon; therm; chron; 3. put a damper on things – upset everyone; put all of my eggs in one basket – put all of your resources into one thing

Answer Key

Page 53
Day 1: 1. Answers will vary but may include he was a hard worker. 2. a pass through the Sierra Nevada Mountains; **Day 2:** 1–4. Answers will vary. Check students' work. **Day 3:** 1. anti; 2. de; 3. dis; 4. in; 5. im; 6. over; 7. sub; 8. un; **Day 4:** 1. Yes. She was on cloud nine. Everyone was complimenting her. 2. underlined: on cloud nine, was speechless, It's raining cats and dogs, keep an eye on everyone, slower than molasses; Answers will vary but may include wanting to make the text more interesting.

Page 54
1. Check students' work. 2. fore; ir; pre; re; super; semi; under; mid; 3. Always be prepared for the unexpected. Answers will vary.

Page 55
Day 1: 1. the United States government; 2. Oklahoma; 3. underlined: Answers will vary but should reference how hard and sad the trip was. **Day 2:** 1–3. Check students' work. **Day 3:** 1. able; 2. est; 3. ful; 4. ing; 5. tion; 6. ity; 7. less; 8. ly; **Day 4:** 1. first person; underlined: I , me; 2. Answers will vary but may include Brooke questioning why the author lied.

Page 56
1. Check students' work. 2. ible; al; en; er; ness; ous; es; y; 3. hold a candle to; out of the blue; one-track mind; foot in my mouth

Page 57
Day 1: 1. a story told through many generations; 2. The chiefs asked the Great One for a sign. **Day 2:** 1. A; 2. B; **Day 3:** 1. water; 2. sound; 3. shape; 4. break; 5. judge; 6. many; 7. write; 8. look; **Day 4:** 1. without stopping; 2. Answers will vary but may include determined.

Page 58
1. C; 2. Check students' work. 3. Answers will vary but should include details from the text. 4. Check students' work.

Page 59
Day 1: 1. George Washington; 2. Answers will vary but should include teaching himself to read or leaving home at 10. 3. Answers will vary but may include independent. **Day 2:** 1–3. Answers will vary. Check students' work. **Day 3:** 1. self; 2. life; 3. time; 4. thing written; 5. writing; 6. water; 7. study of; 8. small; **Day 4:** 1. food as prey; 2. Yes; It is an insect.

Page 60
1–2. Check students' work. 3. The leaves close quickly after trapping the prey. Answers will vary but may include an illustration to help explain the process.

Page 61
Day 1: underlined: Answers will vary but should reference that he refused to give up and discovered more than 300 uses for the peanut plant. 2. It helped farmers. **Day 2:** 1–3. Answers will vary. Check students' work. **Day 3:** 1. one; 2. shape; 3. fear; 4. sound; 5. light; 6. spirit; 7. viewing instrument; 8. heat; **Day 4:** 1. Answers will vary but may include a rabbit. underlined: ears, soft and tall; nose, pink and small; 2. in love; 3. poem

Page 62
1–2. Check students' work. 3. Answers will vary but should include determination.

Page 63
Day 1: 1. B; 2. Veterans Day; **Day 2:** 1–3. Check students' work. **Day 3:** 1. against; 2. opposite; 3. not; 4. before; 5. middle; 6. not; 7. before; 8. again; **Day 4:** 1. Answers will vary but may include a squirrel. underlined: fuzzy face, acorns you call a treat; 2. Answers will vary but should include being upset. 3. climb quickly

Page 64
1–2. Check students' work. 3. They decorated the graves of soldiers to honor those who gave their lives for freedom. Answers will vary.

Answer Key

Page 65
Day 1: 1. Answers will vary but may include small and hairless. 2. C; **Day 2:** 1. IM; 2. E; 3. D; 4. I; 5. E; 6. I; 7. D; 8. I; **Day 3:** 1. can be; 2. more or one who does; 3. the most; 4. full of; 5. act; 6. without; 7. state of being; 8. more than one; **Day 4:** 1. She was scared and hurt. 2. permission

Page 66
1. I; D; IM; E; IM; 2. Check students' work. 3. Its venom cannot kill humans. the venom

Page 67
Day 1: 1. a bee sting; 2. B; 3. shy or timid; **Day 2:** 1. lightest; 2. cute; 3. bigger; 4. Light; 5. cutest; 6. bigger; 7. lightest; 8. more; 9. louder; **Day 3:** 1. S; 2. H; 3. A; 4. S; 5. A; 6. H; 7. H; 8. S; **Day 4:** 1. Answers will vary but should reference her dishonesty. 2. Answers will vary but may include no because she will probably have a makeup test.

Page 68
1–2. Check students' work. 3. stiff leg hairs; Its hairs may fly into the air and hurt you.

Page 69
Day 1: 1. They guided ships away from dangerous points in the water. 2. continuing with lots of force; **Day 2:** 1. S; 2. S; 3. C; 4. S; 5. C; 6. C; **Day 3:** 1. H; 2. S; 3. S; 4. A; 5. A; 6. S; 7. A; 8. A; **Day 4:** 1. to look like the peacocks; 2. He tied their feathers to his tail.

Page 70
1–2. Answers will vary. 3. Answers will vary but may include that you need to be proud of who you are.

Page 71
Day 1: 1–2. Answers will vary. **Day 2:** 1. but; 2. Neither; nor; 3. but; 4. or; 5. either; or; **Day 3:** 1. A; 2. S; 3. S; 4. H; 5. H; 6. H; 7. H; 8. A; **Day 4:** 1. worried; 2. so he can eat it

Page 72
1–3. Check students' work.

Page 73
Day 1: 1. the parts of the cerebrum; 2. it is gray and wrinkled; **Day 2:** 1. as long as; 2. because; 3. after; 4. until; 5. while; **Day 3:** 1–5. Check students' work. **Day 4:** 1. large; 2. His shadow looked so big.

Page 74
1. CD; CD; S; 2. immense; exclaimed; puny; looked; 3. gave examples of activities that require deep thinking; Check students' work.

Page 75
Day 1: 1. B; 2. holidays to remember those who fought to preserve freedom; **Day 2:** 1. underlined: around; circled: sun; 2. underlined: in; circled: moon; 3. underlined: near; circled: Earth; 4. underlined: on; circled: Mars; 5. underlined: at; circled: Venus; 6. underlined: in; circled: solar system; 7. underlined: through; circled: telescope; 8. underlined: in; circled; night sky; 9. underlined: behind; circled; clouds; 10. underlined; around; circled; a ring; **Day 3:** 1–4. Check students' work. **Day 4:** 1. arguing; 2. his glossy, spotted coat

Page 76
1. Check students' work. 2. Words that are spelled the same but have different meanings. Words that are pronounced the same but are spelled differently and have different meanings. 3. People decorated graves of those who had died during the Civil War. where something began

Page 77
Day 1: 1. a time when spirits created the world; 2. Yes, the stories are passed on to younger generations. **Day 2:** 1. underlined: beneath the frothing waves; circled: beneath; 2. underlined: around the crowded, noisy room; circled: around; 3. underlined: across the street; circled: across; 4. underlined: through the yard; circled: through;

CD-104981 • © Carson-Dellosa

Answer Key

5. underlined: over the high fence; circled: over; 6. underlined: outside at the late recess; circled: outside; 7. underlined: up that steep hill; circled: up; 8. underlined: underneath the small bookcase; circled: underneath; 9. underlined: out of the scary moviet; circled: out; 10. underlined: down the deep well; circled: down; **Day 3:** 1–4. Check students' work. **Day 4:** 1. It is hard to resist watching a good meal. 2. There is safety in numbers.

Page 78
1. underlined; in the chilled bowl; circled: in; underlined: on my bed; circled: on; 2. Check students' work. 3. to keep telling the stories; Check students' work.

Page 79
Day 1: 1. the beginning; 2. for special ceremonies; **Day 2:** 1. a small, red purse; 2. the large, purple slide; 3. pretty, small, brown puppy; 4. delicious red apple; 5. old, round, blue plate; **Day 3:** 1–3. Check students' work. **Day 4:** 1. clever; 2. Answers will vary but should include he was foolish.

Page 80
1. Check students' work. 2. M; S; 3. Check students' work.

Page 81
Day 1: 1. someone who is good at sewing; 2. They could make quilts for their owners.
Day 2: 1–10. Check students' work.
Day 3: 1–3. Check students' work.
Day 4: 1. Answers will vary but should include working hard. 2. did everything she could

Page 82
1. Check students' work. 2. S; M; 3. quilts that told the histories of families; Check students' work.

Page 83
Day 1: 1. a group of people who helped slaves escape to freedom; 2. the places where the slaves stopped for help; **Day 2:** 1–3. Check students' work. **Day 3:** 1. B; 2. C; 3. A; 4. D;

Day 4: 1. It looked nice and green and seemed like a good place to feed in. 2. where you live normally

Page 84
1. Check students' work. 2. Don't wait to do something if you can do it now. 3. Be happy where you are. Check students' work.

Page 85
Day 1: 1. She escaped slavery herself. 2. They helped guide escaping slaves and gave them supplies. **Day 2:** 1. When will you get home? 2. Callista said Mr. Taylor said to do Lesson Eight for homework. 3. Careful, the path is very muddy. 4. At the M.L.K. school, everybody reads Isabelle Allende in sixth grade. 5. I want to read my book all day tomorrow. **Day 3:** 1. B; 2. D; 3. E; 4. A; 5. C; **Day 4:** 1. very upset; 2. C

Page 86
1. Mom yelled, "Be nice to your sister!" 2. We always think others have it better than we do. 3. Check students' work.

Page 87
Day 1: 1. choices that are important; 2. choices can either make the world better for everyone or better for just themselves; **Day 2:** 1. Oh, no! There has been an accident! 2. "Can Lynn come over after school?" I asked. 3. Tony and Wren wanted to go to the movies. 4. "I don't know how to do this," Zack complained. 5. "Hey! Be careful!" Quinn yelled. **Day 3:** 1. C; 2. B; 3. E; 4. A; 5. D;
Day 4: 1. to gain the admiration of; 2. Answers will vary but should include not being prideful.

Page 88
1. Jeremy wanted to go to the store, but Irene wanted to go to the restaurant. 2. I'm listening. Go to bed. 3. He kept working to free slaves even though it cost him.

Notes